Moving Into the Future

National Physical Education Standards:
A Guide to Content and Assessment

National Association for Sport & Physical Education

Developed by the
National Association for Sport and Physical Education

WCB McGraw-Hill

Boston, Massachusetts   Burr Ridge, Illinios   Dubuque, Iowa
Madison, Wisconsin   New York, New York   San Francisco, California   St. Louis, Missouri

**National
Association
for Sport &
Physical Education**

NASPE is an association of the
American Alliance for Health, Physical Education, Recreation and Dance (AAHPERD)

WCB/McGraw-Hill

A Division of The McGraw·Hill Companies

Designed by Steve Reardon

International Standard Book Number: **0-8151-7338-5**

National Association for Sport and Physical Education

Standards and Assessment Task Force

Judith Rink, *Professor of Physical Education, University of South Carolina - Chairperson*
Charles Dotson, *Professor of Physical Education, University of Maryland*
Marian Franck, *Physical Education Specialist, Lancaster, Pennsylvania*
Larry Hensley, *Professor of Physical Education, University of Northern Iowa*
Shirley Holt-Hale, *Physical Education Specialist, Oak Ridge, Tennessee*
Jacalyn Lund, *Professor Physical Education, University of Louisville*
Greg Payne, *Professor of Physical Education, San Jose State University*
Terry Wood, *Professor of Physical Education, Oregon State University*

Staff:
Charlene R. Burgeson, *Program Administrator*
Judith C. Young, *Executive Director*

About the cover...

The figure on the cover is a solid geometric shape called an icosahedron. It has 20 sides and provides a basis for the symbolic representation of human movement, called labanotation. The human figure inside the icosahedron demonstrates that the motion of a person can be described by using the planes of the shape as reference points in describing range, direction, quality and form of physical movement. This symbolic description allows the recording of movement patterns so that they may be repeated later or learned by multiple performers. We have based the design of this book on the icosahedron because such recording of movement in order to reproduce performance is especially important in sports such as dance, figure skating, gymnastics, diving and synchronized swimming, but could also be used to describe **any** movement.

Contents

Preface

The National Association for Sport and Physical Education appointed the Outcomes Committee to answer the question "What should students know and be able to do?" The "Outcomes Project" culminated in the development of a definition of the physically educated person. This definition included five major focus areas, specifying that a physically educated person:

- Has learned skills necessary to perform a variety of physical activities
- Is physically fit
- Does participate regularly in physical activity
- Knows the implications of and the benefits from involvement in physical activities
- Values physical activity and its contribution to a healthful lifestyle

This definition was expanded to twenty outcome statements and then further expanded into sample benchmarks for selected grade levels. The work of this committee resulted in the publication of the *Outcomes of Quality Physical Education Programs* (1992). Following this publication, the Standards and Assessment Task Force was appointed to develop content standards and assessment material based on the outcomes document.

The work of the task force, which began in the Spring of 1992, reflects the national education reform movements, particularly with the efforts to establish national content standards for each of the areas of the school curriculum. This movement to clarify and establish important educational goals has provided the impetus and direction for much of the work of the Physical Education Standards and Assessment Task Force. To make the materials for physical education parallel to the materials being developed by other content areas, the identification of "content standards" and the further clarification of the content in physical education were undertaken before the issue of assessment was addressed. The "content standards" and accompanying assessment guidelines have been designed to expand and compliment, not replace, the physical education outcomes document.

This document is the result of a purposeful process of consensus-building that has included a variety of efforts designed to obtain a broad range of expertise and reaction. This work includes the input of many NASPE members and structures (i.e., Council on Physical Education for Children, Middle and Secondary School Physical Education Council, Curriculum and Instruction Academy). The process has also included presentations at both the 1993 and 1994 national AAHPERD conventions, presentations at each of the six district AAHPERD conventions, many state AAHPERD meetings, a review by selected leaders in the physical education profession, as well as consultation with educational representatives from other subject areas (mathematics, arts, science) and educational organizations (Council of Chief State School Officers, Principal's Association, Association of Colleges of Teacher Education).

Although this document is based on input from hundreds of physical education professionals throughout the country, the most important contributions to the preparation of this document come from the members of the Standards and Assessment Task Force. These individuals bring a diversity of expertise to the development of the physical education standards and include both elementary and secondary physical education teachers, authorities in curriculum and pedagogy, as well as measurement and evaluation specialists. Some are experienced authors, others are innovative researchers and teachers, and all are involved in activities that keep them on the "cutting-edge" of physical education.

Introduction

Standards and Educational Reform

Will our children be ready to meet the demands of the 21st century? What do children need to know and be able to do in order to prepare for their futures? These questions and others have prompted parents, educators, business leaders, and politicians to take a hard look at the education system in America. As a result, American education is undergoing an unprecedented reform in an effort to ensure that graduates will be prepared to take their place in society and be able to compete in a global economy. Educational reform received support at the highest levels of government when the President and the nation's governors met at an historic Education Summit in 1989. This led to the announcement of education goals for the nation and the establishment of the National Education Goals Panel to measure progress towards these goals. Emerging from these efforts has been a movement to establish nation-wide education standards. The national standards movement does not approach the task of educational reform through the establishment of a national curriculum or a predetermined course of study, rather they speak of competencies, defining *what a student should know and be able to do.* This represents a new way of thinking, a paradigm shift, about American students. The expectation is that students in every school should be able to reach these standards with adequate support and sustained effort. With the passage of *Goals 2000: Educate America Act* in March 1994, educational standards were written into federal law. Title II of the Act addressed the issue of standards. It establishes a National Education Standards Improvement Council (NESIC), which has, among its other responsibilities, the job of working with appropriate organizations to determine the criteria for certifying voluntary content standards, with three objectives in mind: (1) to ensure that the standards are internationally competitive, (2) to ensure they reflect the best knowledge about teaching and learning, and (3) to ensure they have been developed through a broad-based, open adoption process. In effect, standards have become the cornerstone of the educational reform movement.

The emerging framework suggests two kinds of education standards: content and performance standards. Discovering that there is not clear agreement on definitions of these types of standards, the Technical Planning Group of the National Education Goals Panel sought to provide specific descriptions of each type of standard.

<u>**Content Standards**</u>. Content standards specify "what students should know and be able to do." They include the knowledge and skills—the ways of thinking, communicating, reasoning, and investigating, and the most important enduring ideas, concepts, issues, dilemmas, and information that characterize each discipline. In effect, they involve the knowledge and skills essential to a discipline that students are expected to learn.

<u>**Performance Standards.**</u> Performance standards specify "how good is good enough." They indicate the levels of achievement that students are expected to attain in the content standards. A performance standard indicates both the nature of the evidence (such as an essay, mathematical proof, scientific experiment, project, exam, or combination of these) required to demonstrate that a content standard has been met and the quality of student performance that is deemed acceptable. Performance standards are inextricably tied to issues of assessment.

The report of the Technical Planning Group notes that such performance standards linked to content standards are not yet available. Professional organizations developing standards are concentrating their efforts on specifying what students should know and be able to do. It is recommended that content standards be developed to include examples of possible assessment activities and the specification of the nature of the evidence proposed as necessary to show that the content standards are met. The specification of performance standards could then be part of a process whereby assessments of student work (performance) regularly collected over time would be part of the bases for establishing performance levels. Finally, the term, **performance benchmark**, is used to describe behavior that indicates progress toward a performance standard.

The New Vision of Assessment

Standards-based reform seeks to establish clear, attainable standards at internationally competitive levels for all students throughout America. Because the standards are consensus statements about what a student should "know and be able to do," they provide a basis for student assessment, and for evaluating programs, at national, state, and local levels. Assessment is the process of gathering evidence about a student's level of achievement in a specified subject area and of making inferences based on that evidence for a variety of purposes. Educators must be able to assess individual achievement, otherwise, it will be impossible to know whether the standards are being reached. Whereas a broad range of assessment techniques (measures) could well be used to determine whether a given standard is being met, such assessment should (1) reflect the subject content that is most important for students to learn, (2) enhance learning through a connection with instruction, (3) provide consistent (reliable) evidence of student performance, and (4) yield valid inferences about student learning. In effect, assessment serves to undergird the standards movement. It is the "glue" that holds the standards framework together.

A significant benefit to physical education offered through the delineation of a comprehensive set of standards and accompanying assessments is that they combat the uninformed idea that physical education is an "academically soft" area of study. The standards essentially say that physical education has academic standing. They say there is such a thing as achievement, that knowledge and skills matter, and that mere willing participation is not the same as education. They affirm that discipline and rigor are essential to achievement. And they further state that all behaviors associated with physical education can in some way be measured—if not always on a numerical scale, then by informed critical judgment.

At a time in which greater demands are likely to be placed on assessment than any time in the history of American education, there is growing dissatisfaction with the traditional forms of assessment, whether it is the use of multiple-choice, machine-scored tests or the use of standardized sport skill of physical fitness tests. Although many physical education teachers use a variety of tests, and there are hundreds of tests to choose from, to measure attributes such as physical fitness or sport skill competency, they frequently feel dissatisfied with what these tests reflect. They know that students are learning, yet the use of these tests don't seem to facilitate learning nor provide a very good indicator of what was learned. Furthermore, many of the available techniques and tests are impractical to use in the typical physical education class setting and are not conducive to enhancing instruction. Perhaps no other element of the instructional process is so often abused as the assessment process.

Amid the dissatisfaction and controversy over assessment procedures, the reform movement in education includes changing assessment to a program that is more fully integrated with the teaching process and provides meaningful information about student learning and achievement. The transformation of assessment programs, especially the day-to-day teacher initiated assessment, is toward performance-based assessments that focus on high-priority objectives and significant outcomes for students. Such performance assessment usually refers to assessment tasks in which students demonstrate skills and competencies rather than selecting one of several predetermined answers to an exercise. Furthermore, assessments that are "authentic" in nature, that is, designed to take place in a real-life setting rather than in an artificial or contrived setting, are being advocated. While this movement towards authentic assessment is being heralded as innovative, in reality many of these assessment techniques have been used in physical education for years. The very nature of the content of physical education frequently manifests itself in directly observable behavior. As a result, observational analysis and subjective methods of assessment have frequently used by physical education teachers. The current interest in performance-based authentic assessment seems to provide legitimacy to many of these methods.

Although the assessment process may be utilized by teachers and school officials for many discrete tasks, too often assessment is seen solely for the purpose of determining a student grade. To narrowly identify grading as the singular purpose of assessment is a significant factor contributing to inappropriate assessment practices and poor instruction in general. The primary goal of assessment should be seen as the enhancement of learning, rather than simply the documentation of learning. The assessment model therefore becomes formative in nature, placing teachers' professional judgments at the center of the process. The process itself may be more informal, practical, and expedient, as well as more relaxed in terms of psychometric standards. It is within this context that the various assessment options presented herein have been developed.

For all students to become physically educated, assessment practices must support the instruction of physical education and the learning of each student. This is the primary goal of assessment in school physical education. When done equitably, assessment of student progress will further learning. Assessment should be a dynamic process that continuously yields information about student progress toward the achievement of the content standards in physical education. The process of gathering evidence to make inferences about student learning communicates to students and all of those concerned with their learning what is valued in physical education and how students are progressing toward specific goals. When the information gathered is consistent with learning goals and is used appropriately to guide teaching, it can enhance learning as well as document it. Unless we embrace a new philosophy of assessment and implement new assessment activities geared to high-priority objectives, physical education will fall short of achieving new visions of excellence as sought in educational reform.

The Standards

The purpose of this document is to:

- establish **content standards** for the physical education school program that clearly identify consensus statements related to what a student should know and be able to do as a result of a quality physical education program, and,

- establish teacher-friendly **guidelines for assessment** of the content standards that are consistent with instructionally integrated orientations the role of assessment in the teaching/learning process.

The development of the content standards and accompanying assessment guide was most influenced by (a) the previous work of the NASPE Outcomes Committee, (b) the national standards movement in educational reform, and (c) the newer vision of the role of assessment in the teaching/learning process.

A general description of each content standard is first presented, followed by presentation of the standards according to grade level: K, 2, 4, 6, 8, 10, and 12. Since the primary users of the standards will be teachers and educational administrators, the standards are presented according to grade level, a format being followed by other subject areas. Within each grade level, the standard is further defined, followed by a listing of the key points of emphasis for that grade level. Sample performance benchmarks, which describe developmentally appropriate behaviors representative of progress toward achieving the standard, are also presented. Lastly, a variety of assessment techniques appropriate for assessing student achievement of the specified content standard is described. This includes specific examples of selected assessment options accompanied by illustrative criteria recommended for the assessment technique described. The assessment examples provided herein are just that, examples; they are not meant to be a comprehensive listing of available assessment techniques, nor are they meant to be the "best" assessment techniques to be used in all situations. The examples provided are illustrative of numerous performance assessments and authentic assessments that may be used to make inferences about student learning.

Content Standards in Physical Education

A physically educated person:

1. Demonstrates competency in many movement forms and proficiency in a few movement forms.

2. Applies movement concepts and principles to the learning and development of motor skills.

3. Exhibits a physically active lifestyle.

4. Achieves and maintains a health-enhancing level of physical fitness.

5. Demonstrates responsible personal and social behavior in physical activity settings.

6. Demonstrates understanding and respect for differences among people in physical activity settings.

7. Understands that physical activity provides opportunities for enjoyment, challenge, self-expression, and social interaction.

General Description of Standards

1. Demonstrates competency in many movement forms and proficiency in a few movement forms

The intent of this standard is the development of movement competence and proficiency. Movement competence implies the development of sufficient ability to enjoy participation in physical activities and establishes a foundation to facilitate continued motor skill acquisition and increased ability to engage in appropriate motor patterns in daily physical activities. The development of proficiency in a few movement forms gives the student the capacity for successful and advanced levels of performance to further increase the likelihood of participation. In the primary years students develop maturity and versatility in the use of fundamental skills (e.g., running, skipping, throwing, striking) that are further refined, combined and varied during the middle school years. These motor patterns, now having evolved into specialized skills (e.g., a specific dance step, chest pass, catching with a glove) are used in increasingly more complex movement environments (e.g., more players or participants, rules, and strategies) through the middle school years. On the basis of interest and ability, high school students select a few activities for regular participation within which proficiency will be developed. In preparation for adulthood, students should have acquired the basic skills to participate in a wide variety of leisure and work-related physical activities and advanced skills in at least two or three areas.

2. Applies movement concepts and principles to the learning and development of motor skills

This standard concerns the ability of the learner to use cognitive information to understand and enhance motor skill acquisition and performance. This includes the application of concepts from disciplines such as motor learning and development, sport psychology and sociology, biomechanics, and exercise physiology. Specifically this would include concepts like increasing force production through the summation of forces, effects of anxiety on performance, and the principle of specificity of training. Knowledge of such concepts and practice applying these concepts enhances the likelihood of independent learning and therefore more regular and effective participation in physical activity. During the lower elementary years emphasis is placed on establishing a movement vocabulary and initial application of introductory concepts (e.g., force absorption, principles governing equilibrium, application of force). Through the upper elementary and middle school years an emphasis is placed on learning more and increasingly complex concepts. In addition, emphasis is placed on applying and generalizing these concepts to real-life physical activity situations (e.g., managing stress, effect of growth spurt on movement performance). During the high school years the student should possess sufficient knowledge of concepts to independently and routinely use a wide variety of increasingly complex concepts (e.g., performance trends associated with learning new motor skills, specificity of training). By graduation the student should have developed sufficient knowledge and ability to independently use their knowledge to acquire new skills while continuing to refine existing ones.

3. Exhibits a physically active lifestyle

The intent of this standard is to establish patterns of regular participation in meaningful physical activity. This standard should connect what is done in the physical education class with the lives of students outside of physical education. While participation within the physical education class is important, what the student does outside the physical education class is critical to developing an active, healthy lifestyle. Students are more likely to participate if they have had opportunities to develop interests that are personally meaningful to them. Young children should learn to enjoy physical activity. They should participate in developmentally appropriate activities that help them develop movement competence and they should be encouraged to participate in vigorous and unstructured play. As students get older the structure of activity tends to increase and the opportunities for participation in different types of activity increase outside of the physical education class. Attainment of this standard should develop an awareness of those opportunities and encourage a broad level of participation. Cognitive understandings develop from an initial awareness of cause and effect relationships between activity and its immediate and identifiable effects on the body to an increased understanding of the role of physical activity on the physiological body, social opportunities and relationships, and emotional well being; and a comprehensive perspective on the meaning of the idea of a healthy lifestyle.

4. Achieves and maintains a health-enhancing level of physical fitness

The intent of this standard is for the student to achieve a health-enhancing level of physical fitness. Students should be encouraged to develop higher levels of basic fitness and physical competence as needed for many work situations and active leisure participation. Health-related fitness components include cardiorespiratory endurance, muscular strength and endurance, flexibility, and body composition. Expectations for students' fitness levels should be established on a personal basis, taking into account variation in entry levels, rather than setting a single standards for all children at a given grade level. For elementary children, the emphasis is on an awareness of fitness components and having fun while participating in health-enhancing activities that promote physical fitness. Middle school students gradually acquire a greater understanding of the fitness components, how each is developed and maintained, and the importance of each in overall fitness. Secondary students are able to design and develop an appropriate personal fitness program that enables them to achieve desired levels of fitness. The student thus should have both the ability and willingness to accept responsibility for personal fitness leading to an active, healthy lifestyle.

5. Demonstrates responsible personal and social behavior in physical activity settings

The intent of this standard is achievement of self-initiated behaviors that promote personal and group success in activity settings. These include safe practices, adherence to rules and procedures, etiquette, cooperation and teamwork, ethical behavior in sport, and positive social interaction. Achievement of this standard in the lower elementary grades begins with recognition of classroom rules and procedures and a focus on safety. In the upper elementary levels, students learn to work independently, with a partner, and in small groups. In the middle school, students identify the purposes for rules and procedures and become involved in decision making processes to establish rules and procedures for specific activity situations. High school students initiate responsible behavior, function independently and responsibly, and positively influence the behavior of others in physical activity settings.

6. Demonstrates understanding and respect for differences among people in physical activity settings

The intent of this standard is to develop respect for individual similarities and differences through positive interaction among participants in physical activity. Similarities and differences include characteristics of culture, ethnicity, motor performance, disabilities, physical characteristics (e.g., strength, size, shape), gender, race, and socio-economic status. Elementary school students begin to recognize individual similarities and differences and participate cooperatively in physical activity. By middle school, students participate cooperatively in physical activity with persons of diverse characteristics and backgrounds. High school students are expected to be able to participate with all people, recognize the value of diversity in physical activity, and develop strategies for inclusion of others.

7. Understands that physical activity provides opportunities for enjoyment, challenge, self-expression, and social interaction

This standard is designed to develop an awareness of the intrinsic values and benefits of participation in physical activity that provides personal meaning. Physical activity can provide opportunity for self-expression and social interaction and can be enjoyable, challenging, and fun. These benefits entice people to continue participation in activity throughout the life span. Elementary school children derive pleasure from movement sensations and experience challenge and joy as they sense a growing competence in movement ability. At the middle school level participation in physical activity provides important opportunities for challenge, social interaction, and group membership, as well as opportunities for continued personal growth in physical skills and their applied settings. Participation at the high school level continues to provide enjoyment and challenge as well as opportunities for self-expression and social interaction. As a result of these intrinsic benefits of participation, students will begin to actively pursue lifelong physical activities that meet their own needs.

Kindergarten

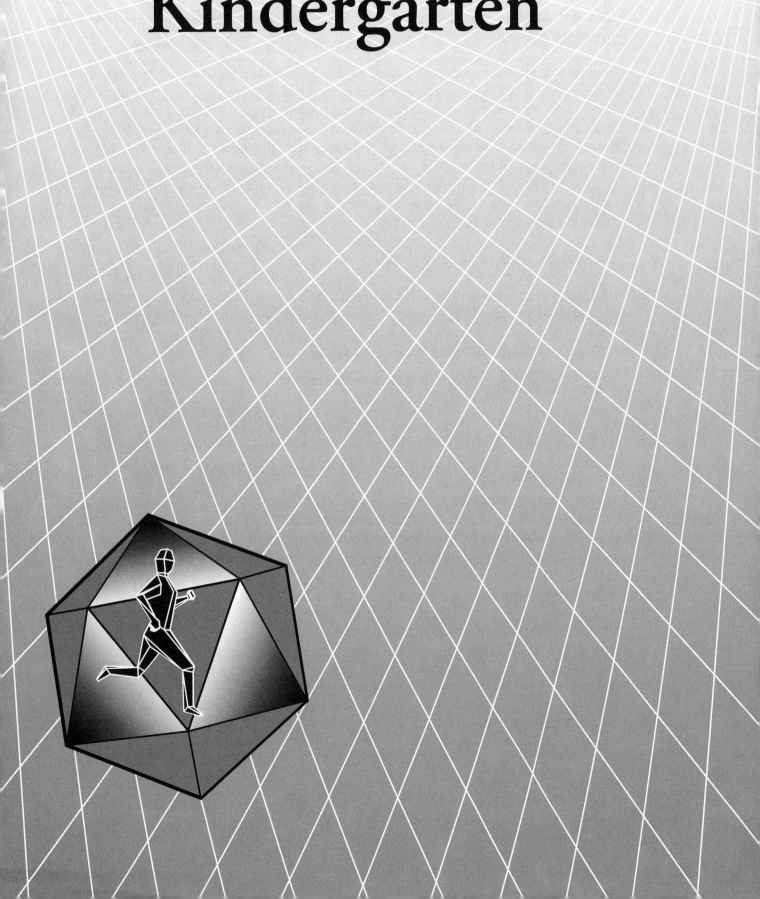

Kindergarten

> **1. Demonstrates competency in many movement forms and proficiency in a few movement forms.**

In most fundamental patterns (e.g., catching, jumping, striking) students are evolving from varying levels of maturity and should be developing the ability to control the use of a pattern. In most fundamental patterns and basic movement skills (e.g., weight bearing, turning, twisting) students can be expected to demonstrate continuous progress toward mature status in the simplest of conditions (e.g., tossing a ball to a close stationary target, jumping down from a low box, taking weight momentarily on hands and landing softly, walking in different directions to the beat of a clear even rhythm). Most kindergarten students can be expected to achieve maturity in walking and running by the end of the school year.

The emphasis for the kindergarten student will be to:

•   Demonstrate progress toward the mature form of selected manipulative, locomotor and nonlocomotor skills.

•   Demonstrate mature form in walking and running.

Sample Benchmarks:

1. Travels in forward and sideways directions using a variety of locomotor (non-locomotor) patterns and changes direction quickly in response to a signal.
2. Demonstrates clear contrasts between slow and fast movement while traveling.
3. Walks and runs using mature form.
4. Rolls sideways without hesitating or stopping.
5. Tosses a ball and catches it before it bounces twice.
6. Kicks a stationary ball using a smooth continuous running step.
7. Maintains momentary stillness bearing weight on a variety of body parts.

Assessment Examples:

1. Teacher observation - observational record

The student will be asked to travel through general space with a steady run, and upon a designated signal, perform the next locomotor action announced by the teacher (e.g., walk, hop, gallop). Upon observing the student's performance, the teacher marks on a checklist mastery of the various critical elements (e.g., arm swing, balance, foot placement).

Criteria for Assessment:
a. Demonstrates selected critical elements of locomotor skills
b. Responds with correct locomotor skill as named by teacher

2. Written test

Students are provided a drawing of an underhand and an overhand throwing pattern and asked to circle the overhand throwing pattern.

Students are provided a drawing of different pathways—straight, curved, zigzag—and asked to identify the pathway named by the teacher.

Criteria for Assessment:
  a. Correctly identifies the movement pattern or concept

3. Event task - observational record

Students will perform a "Dance of Locomotors" in which they travel in different ways through general space. Upon hearing a designated signal from the teacher, students will change to the locomotor pattern named by the teacher. Repeat the dance, but this time upon the signal to change locomotor pattern the students will respond by selecting any locomotor pattern they desire. The teacher should encourage creative modes of travel.

Criteria for Assessment:
  a. Demonstrates a variety of locomotor skills
  b. Identifies and models locomotor movements shown by the teacher
  c. Exhibits correct locomotor skill when the skill is named by the teacher

4. Teacher observation - observational record

The teacher uses a checklist to assess the degree to which a class or individual students can identify a "good personal space"; work in "personal space" and move in "general space" during a manipulative lesson.

Criteria for Assessment:
  a. Finds a personal space within general space that provides maximum room to work
  b. Stays in or returns to personal space during lesson
  c. Moves with an awareness of others as well as space available within general space

2. Applies movement concepts and principles to the learning and development of motor skills.

The kindergarten student begins to realize basic cognitive concepts associated with movement and how to use them to guide their performance in games, body management, and dance. For example, the student learns to apply concepts like pathway, level, range, and direction to their locomotor patterns to extend their movement versatility. Through instruction, students can also begin to recognize and apply some characteristics of mature fundamental motor patterns (e.g., taking a step with the leg opposite the

throwing arm, increasing leg flexion in preparation for a jump).

The emphasis for the kindergarten student will be to:

- Identify fundamental movement patterns (skip, strike).

- Establish a beginning movement vocabulary (e.g., personal space, high/low levels, fast/slow speeds, light/heavy weights, balance, twist).

- Apply appropriate concepts to performance (e.g., change direction while running).

Sample Benchmarks:

1. Walks, runs, hops, and skips, in forward and sideways directions, and changes direction quickly in response to a signal.
2. Identifies and uses a variety of relationships with objects (e.g., over/under, behind, alongside, through).
3. Identifies and begins to utilize the technique employed (leg flexion) to soften the landing in jumping.

Assessment Examples:

1. Teacher observation - observational record

Students will play a game of "Follow the Leader" in which the teacher demonstrates a locomotor movement and then observes the students to determine if they can replicate the action as demonstrated. The teacher varies the movement by changing the concept applied on each repetition.

Criteria for Assessment:
a. Selects proper body parts, skills, and movement concepts
b. Responds appropriately to a variety of cues

2. Teacher observation - observational record

The students play a game of "Bear Hunt" by performing the actions of a story told by the teacher. A variety of locomotor and nonlocomotor movements should be used. Students should practice the actions before playing the game. The teacher observes the movements of the student for appropriateness of response to the verbal cue.

Criteria for Assessment:
a. Applies movement concepts while practicing basic movements
b. Selects proper body parts, skills, and movement concepts
c. Responds appropriately to a variety of cues

3. Student project

Students are asked to pretend they are recreating the story of Jack and Jill rolling down the hill. They can pretend they are Jack and/or Jill and describe and demonstrate what Jack and Jill would need to do to roll sideways down the hill. The student prepares a drawing that illustrates the rolling action used by Jack and Jill.

Criteria for Assessment:
a. Identifies the critical elements of rolling
b. Demonstrates appropriate rolling movement

3. Exhibits a physically active lifestyle.

The intent of this standard is to develop positive attitudes toward participation in physical activity and a general awareness that physical activity is both fun and good for you. Students should recognize that participation in moderate to vigorous physical activity has both temporary and lasting positive effects on the body and know that exercise contributes to improved health. A main focus in kindergarten is providing students with sufficient knowledge and understanding of physical activity to develop positive attitudes toward healthy lifestyles and the activities themselves.

The emphasis for the kindergarten student should be to:

• Engage in moderate to vigorous physical activity.

• Select and participate in activities that require some physical exertion during unscheduled times.

• Identify likes and dislikes connected with participation in physical activity.

Sample Benchmarks:

1. Participates regularly in vigorous physical activity.
2. Recognizes that physical activity is good for personal well-being.
3. Identifies feelings that result from participation in physical activities.

Assessment Examples:
1. Teacher observation - observational record

During recess a variety of games with varying degrees of physical exertion are available for the student. Student choices are observed and periodically recorded by the teacher or aides.

Observation Key:
    3= High intensity (e.g., sustained vigorous running or rope jumping leading to

heavy breathing and perspiration)

2=   Medium intensity (e.g., intermittent games or activities leading to occasional increased respiration and some perspiration)

1=   Low intensity (e.g., sedentary games or activities leading to no visible physical change)

0=   No appreciable activity (e.g., standing around)

Criteria for Assessment:
a. Selects activities that are vigorous in nature
b. Participates at a level sufficient to increase breathing and sweating
c. Participates regularly in health-enhancing physical activities

2. Student project

Students participate in a classtime physical activity. At the conclusion, they draw a picture indicating their feelings during and following the activity. Students are asked to explain their drawings to their classmates.

Criteria for Assessment:
a. Identifies feelings following participation in physical activity
b. Communicates likes and dislikes connected with the activity
c. Identifies the physical changes that occur as a result of various physical activities

3. Self-assessment

Students are asked to complete a teacher-made questionnaire (read by the teacher) by circling the appropriate level of smiley face to indicate how much they like a physical activity.

Criteria for Assessment:
a. Identifies feelings following participation in physical activity
b. Differentiates between activities that are more or less pleasurable

4. Achieves and maintains a health-enhancing level of physical fitness.

Kindergarten students enjoy physical activities for the pleasure experienced from simply moving. The focus at this level is on helping students to sustain physical activity intermittently for short periods of time and have fun while doing so. They are able to recognize physiological signs associated with engagement in vigorous physical activity.

The emphasis for the kindergarten student will be to:

• Sustain moderate to vigorous physical activity for short periods of time.

• Identify the physiological signs of moderate physical activity (e.g., fast heart rate,

heavy breathing).

Sample Benchmarks:

1. Sustains moderate to vigorous physical activity.
2. Is aware of his or her heart beating fast during physical activity.

Assessment Examples:

1. Teacher observation - observational record

Have students engage in a series of locomotor actions, e.g., timed segments of hopping, walking, jumping, galloping, running. Observe the class, noting those individuals who appear to tire easily and those unable to sustain activity.

Criteria for Assessment:
a. Stopping the locomotor action before the teacher signals to do so
b. Displays obvious signs of fatigue while continuing the locomotor action

2. Event task - observational record

Have the class participate for several minutes in a vigorous activity, e.g., Sticky Popcorn. Ask them to place hands on chest to feel the heartbeat before the activity and immediately after the activity stops. Lead a class discussion of: (1) What is the difference between your heartbeat before we did the activity and now? (2) Why is your heart beating faster now? (3) Is anyone sweating? (4) What other activities could we do to make our heart beat faster?

Criteria for Assessment:
a. Associates the faster heartbeat with vigorous activity
b. Associates the slower heartbeat with rest
c. Identifies other physical activities that elicit a faster heartbeat

5. Demonstrates responsible personal and social behavior in physical activity settings.

Students begin to learn and utilize acceptable behaviors for physical activity settings. Focus is directed towards understanding safe practices as well as classroom rules and procedures. They begin to understand the concept of cooperation through opportunities to share space and equipment with others in a group.

The emphasis for the kindergarten student will be to:

• Apply, with teacher reinforcement, classroom rules and procedures and safe practices.

- Share space and equipment with others.

Sample Benchmarks:

1. Knows the rules for participating in the gymnasium and on the playground.
2. Works in a group setting without interfering with others.
3. Responds to teacher signals for attention.
4. Responds to rule infractions when reminded once.
5. Follows directions given to the class for an all-class activity.
6. Handles equipment safely by putting it away when not in use.
7. Takes turns using a piece of equipment.
8. Transfers rules of the gym to "rules of the playground."

Assessment Examples:

1. Teacher observation - observational record

The teacher records the names of students who had to be reminded of rules and procedures after each class period and those who do not respond after being reminded. The teacher initiates individual attention to those students who do not respond after being reminded once.

Criteria for Assessment:
a. Complies with the rules or procedures established in the class
b. Complies after being reminded of a rule or procedure
c. Is able to explain the questioned behavior and establish the expected behavior

2. Teacher observation - observational record

After the rules and procedures have been taught, the teacher checks for understanding by having the children play the "Number Game." Students are asked to act out the rule when given by the teacher. The teacher counts to see how long it takes all children to follow the rule stated.

Criteria for Assessment:
a. Responds accurately to the identified rules and procedures
b. Responds quickly to the teacher's signals

3. Student project - observational record

Students are asked to select a picture, from a group of examples provided by the teacher, of one way in which they can share space and equipment with others in an activity.

Criteria for Assessment:
a. Accurately identifies a characteristic of sharing
b. Explains the importance of the selected characteristic of sharing

6. Demonstrates understanding and respect for differences among people in physical activity settings

Students in kindergarten are primarily concerned with how the world relates to them as individuals and are beginning to be aware of the relationships with others. They are discovering the joy of playing with friends and how social interaction can make activities more fun. Social interaction for kindergartners has focused mainly on the family. Physical education helps expand this world.

The emphasis for the kindergarten student will be to:

• Recognize the joy of shared play.

• Interact positively with students in class regardless of personal differences (e.g., race, gender, disability).

Sample Benchmarks:

1. Enjoys participation alone and with others.
2. Chooses playmates without regard to personal differences (e.g., race, gender, disability).

Assessment Examples:

1. Teacher observation - observational record

Students are observed working on tasks both alone and with other students. The student willingly enters into these situations and does not have to be forced to do so by the teacher. When the student participates with others, there is group harmony. When disputes arise, the students are able to resolve the difficulty and continue to work together. The student also demonstrates these behaviors during unstructured time and recess time.

Criteria for Assessment:
a. Demonstrates willingness to join in the activity
b. Participates in group activities readily as evidenced by the amount of latency between the teacher's instruction and the time activity begins.
c. Demonstrates cooperation with others in group tasks.

2. Interview

Following a group or partner game or activity, students (as a group or individually) are asked to verbalize the similarities and differences in participating alone versus with a group or partner.

Criteria for Assessment:
a. Recognizes that participation with a partner/group requires sharing and cooperation
b. Recognizes that sharing with others can lead to positive feelings such as feelings of acceptance and belonging to the group

> **7. Understands that physical activity provides the opportunity for enjoyment, challenge, self-expression, and social interaction.**

It is evidenced by their smiles and actions that kindergarten children enjoy participating in physical education activities. Movement does not have to occur in structured games or competitive situations to be fun for them. At this level, a child may play within a group, but not necessarily as a member of the group. Kindergartners like the challenge of experiencing new movements and learning new skills.

The emphasis for the kindergarten student will be to:

• Engage in physical activities.

• Associate positive feelings with participation in physical activity.

• Try new movement activities and skills.

Sample Benchmarks:

1. Enjoys participation alone and with others.
2. Identifies feelings that result from participation in physical activities.
3. Looks forward to physical education classes.

Assessment Examples:

1. Teacher observation - observational record

Students are periodically observed during activity within physical education class to ascertain their level of participation and involvement in the chosen activity.

Criteria for Assessment:
a. Demonstrates active involvement in physical activity
b. Smiles and shows both verbal and nonverbal indicators of enjoyment

2. Group project

Students are asked to work together in a group to create a "Physical Education Book" for their classroom. Each child is to draw activities that represent physical education class. With assistance from the classroom teacher, sentences can be added to describe the activity.

Criteria for Assessment:
a. Willingly participates in the project
b. Identifies several activities that are enjoyable
c. Expresses positive feelings when describing the activity

3. Interview - observational record

Classroom teachers often have a brief sharing time after special area classes as a transition back to classroom activities. Ask the teacher to periodically obtain feedback from the children regarding enjoyment of activities by:
a) raising of hands
b) thumbs up, thumbs down
c) verbal comments from children.

Criteria for Assessment:
a. Indicates verbally or nonverbally positive feelings toward physical activity
b. Raises his or her hand to share feelings about physical activity

Second Grade

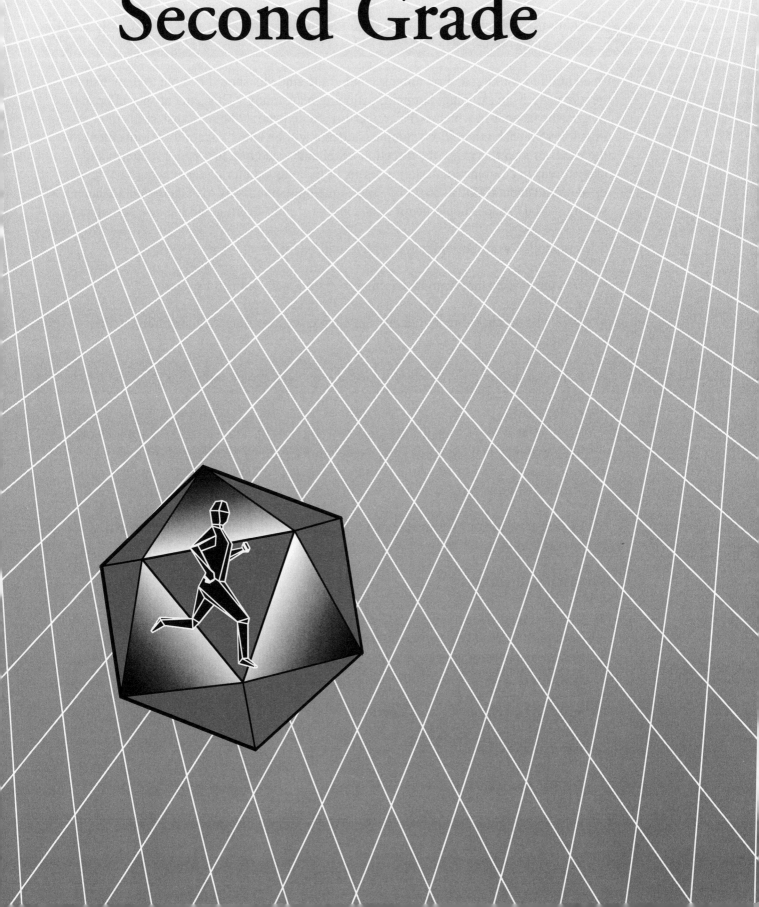

Second Grade

> **1. Demonstrates competency in many movement forms and proficiency in a few movement forms.**

In addition to walking and running, second grade students should be able to demonstrate mature patterns in skipping, hopping, galloping and sliding. This student should be able to vary the manner in which skills are performed and should begin to use skills in combination with each other. For example, students will be able to adapt their movement to the needs of a partner; vary the direction, level and speed of a locomotor pattern; and use patterns in combination. Mature forms of basic locomotor patterns should be developed. Fundamental skills should be used in manipulative, body management and dance settings. Body shape should begin to be clear in weight-bearing and balance activities.

The emphasis for the second grade student will be to:

- Demonstrate mature form in skipping, hopping, galloping and sliding.

- Demonstrate mature motor patterns in simple combinations (e.g, dribbling while running).

- Demonstrate smooth transitions between sequential motor skills (e.g., running into a jump).

- Exhibit the ability to adapt and adjust movement skills to uncomplicated, yet changing, environmental conditions and expectations (e.g., partner needs for force production, tossing a ball to a moving partner, rising and sinking while twisting, using different rhythms).

- Demonstrate control in traveling activities and weight bearing and balance activities on a variety of body parts

Sample Benchmarks:

1. Demonstrates skills of chasing, fleeing, and dodging to avoid others.
2. Combines locomotor patterns in time to music.
3. Balances, demonstrating momentary stillness, in symmetrical and nonsymmetrical shapes on a variety of body parts.
4. Receives and sends an object in a continuous motion.
5. Strikes a ball repeatedly with a paddle.

Assessment Examples:

1. Teacher observation - observational record

Students are requested to demonstrate the skills introduced in class as the teacher

observes their performance and records the satisfactory use of the critical elements of the skills on a checklist.

Criteria for Assessment:
a. Demonstrates critical elements of the selected skills over several trials

2. Event Task - observational record

Students are asked to design and practice a movement sequence of three different loco-motor skills. Following the practice period, students demonstrate their movement sequence for the class.

Criteria for Assessment
a. Demonstrates three different locomotor movements
b. Demonstrates mature pattern of each locomotor skill
c. Demonstrates smooth transitions between locomotor patterns

3. Peer observation

Students are asked to work on balancing on different bases of support (e.g., two hands and one foot, hands and knees, headstand). Students should balance in four different positions, two using symmetrical shapes and two using asymmetrical shapes. Students are asked to draw their favorite symmetrical and asymmetrical balances on paper, label-ing "S" and "A" respectively. Students now select a partner who will observe their bal-ances and then indicate on the paper: (1) if the drawn figures were labeled correctly and (2) if the balances were held still for 3 seconds.

Criteria for Assessment:
a. Completes four balances, two-symmetrical and two-asymmetrical
b. Correctly labels balances "S" and "A"
c. Maintains stillness in balance for three seconds
d. Observer correctly assesses the appropriateness of the labels and the extent to which the performer was still

4. Teacher observation (video) - observational record

Students are asked to skip, gallop, and jump off a low box. A camera is set up in one corner of the gym to record their performance. Each student is asked to go in front of the camera and perform the specified movement patterns. The teacher uses a checklist to assess the extent to which mature and skilled patterns have been attained.

Criteria for Assessment:
a. Exhibits mature form for each of the movement patterns
b. Demonstrates consistent and smooth performance

2. Applies movement concepts and principles to the learning and development of motor skills.

The second grade student should begin to be able to identify critical elements (characteristics of mature performance) for fundamental skills and use them in performance. Emphasis is placed on identification and performance of movement concepts of space, effort, and relationships that vary the quality of movement.

The emphasis for the second grade student will be to:

* Identify the critical elements of basic movement patterns

* Apply movement concepts to a variety of basic skills

* Use feedback to improve performance

Sample Benchmarks:

1. Identifies four characteristics of a mature throw.
2. Uses concepts of space awareness and movement control to run, hop, and skip in different ways in a large group without bumping into others or falling.
3. Identifies and demonstrates the major characteristics of mature walking, running, hopping, and skipping.

Assessment Examples:

1. Peer observation

Using an appropriate size ball, students practice throwing at a target on the wall alternating with a partner in five throw turns. The students should be instructed to concentrate on the critical elements of throwing as taught by the instructor (i.e., ready position, arm preparation, opposite side to the target, step with leg opposite the throwing arm, follow-through, accuracy of throw). After each bout of five throws the partner gives feedback on one of the critical elements by drawing a smiley face on a score sheet each time the element is employed as instructed. Note changes in performance with subsequent five throw bouts.

Criteria for Assessment:
a. Recognizes critical elements of basic movement pattern
b. Adjusts conditions for success following feedback

2. Written test - drawing

Students are provided with a drawing of a hand print and are asked to color the portion of the hand that is used in mature dribbling. Students may also be asked to draw an entire person dribbling to show the overall critical elements of this movement task.

Criteria for Assessment:

a. Correctly identifies portion of hand used in mature dribbling

b. Identifies the critical elements of dribbling

3. Written/oral test

Students are shown photographs of professional dancers, elite gymnasts, or other sport performers in action and are asked to identify the movement patterns they have been studying in class and the critical elements that contribute to successful performance of the movement. Written or oral responses can be solicited.

Criteria for Assessment

a. Identifies the basic movement patterns

b. Identifies the critical elements leading to successful performance

4. Event task

Have the students pretend that Rapunzel recently enrolled in your school. She knows nothing about catching a ball. Students are ask to explain what Rapunzel needs to know to catch a ball thrown to her from the front at about chest height. Instruct the students to imagine themselves practicing with Rapunzel and providing feedback after each attempted catch. Have them imagine looking for the critical elements (ready position, hand and arm position, eye contact, and absorption of force).

Criteria for Assessment:

a. Identifies critical elements of catching

b. Uses appropriate feedback to improve performance

3. Exhibits a physically active lifestyle.

The intent of this standard in the second grade is still on developing positive attitudes toward regular physical activity and its effect on health. By the second grade, students at this age should be able to identify at least one form of exercise associated with each component of health-related fitness. In addition, they should be able to identify social (e.g., cooperation) and psychological contributions of physical activity (e.g., exploring feelings associated with success or failure).

The emphasis for the second grade student will be to:

• Experience and express pleasure from participation in physical activity.

• Engage in moderate to vigorous physical activity outside of physical education class.

• Identify at least one activity associated with each component of health-related physical activity.

Sample Benchmarks:

1. Seeks participation in gross motor activity of a moderate to vigorous nature.
2. Participates in a wide variety of activities that involve locomotion, nonlocomotion, and manipulation of objects outside of physical education class.
3. Willingly completes physical education activity "homework" assignments.

Assessment Examples:

1. Teacher observation - observational record

The teacher identifies and records the names of those students who do not engage in activities (playground or in class) that require sustained moderate physical activity.

Criteria for Assessment:
a. Initiates participation in vigorous activity
b. Sustains vigorous activity for more than ten minutes

2. Student journal

The student practices a teacher-designed exercise or game designed to improve performance on selected manipulative skills. Practice must occur during out-of-class time, at recess or at home, no less than three times per week for a prescribed number of weeks. After each practice session, the student records information on how long (or number of times) they practiced each day.

Criteria for Assessment:
a. Practices at least three times per week
b. Practices at least ten minutes each day

3. Student journal

Students record what they do in their free time after school for a week and indicate which of the activities require moderate to vigorous physical activity. The journal is signed by the parents at the end of the week and returned to class.

 Criteria for Assessment:
a. Lists a reasonable number of activities
b. Accurately lists activities for the individual
c. Correctly identifies those activities that are vigorous

4. Written test

Students take a teacher-prepared test that consists of a set of pictures which illustrate the health benefits of physical activity. For example:

- A smiling child running (makes you feel good.)
- A person visiting the doctor (exercise can prevent some illnesses)
- A group of people being physically active and enjoying themselves (physical activity as a social experience)
- A figure skater, gymnast, dancer, or diver exhibiting their skill (the beauty of movement and the joy of performing or being a spectator)
- A person actively participating in a sport such as basketball, handball, soccer, or tennis (physical activity as a social experience)
- An obese person sitting on the couch watching television. (does not illustrate a benefit of physical activity)

The student's task is to look at each picture and describe how the picture illustrates a benefit of physical activity.

Criteria for Assessment:
a. Correctly identifies those activities associated with health-related activities
b. Correctly identifies the costs and benefits of each activity

4. Achieves and maintains a health-enhancing level of physical fitness.

Students at this age engage in activities in a variety of settings that promote cardiovascular, musculoskeletal, and body composition benefits. Second grade students should be formally introduced to the components of health-related fitness (cardiorespiratory endurance, muscular strength and endurance, flexibility, and body composition). They can sustain moderate to vigorous physical activity for longer periods of time and will more easily recognize physiological indicators of activity.

The emphasis for the second grade student will be to:

- Engage in sustained physical activity that causes an increased heart rate and heavy breathing.

- Recognize the physiological indicators that accompany moderate to vigorous physical activity (e.g. sweating, increased heart rate, heavy breathing).

- Identify the components of health-related physical fitness.

Sample Benchmarks:

1. Sustains activity for longer periods of time while participating in chasing or fleeing, traveling activities in physical education, and/or on the playground.
2. Identifies changes in the body during vigorous physical activity.
3. Supports body weight for climbing, hanging, and momentarily taking weight on hands.
4. Moves each joint through a full range of motion.

Assessment Examples:

1. Teacher observation - observational record

The teacher identifies those students who drop out of activities that require sustained moderate to vigorous physical activity.

Criteria for Assessment:
a. Sustains the physical activity level needed for full participation in the activity
b. Sustains moderate to vigorous physical activity for more than 10 minutes

2. Event task - observational record

Students are introduced to the concept of cardiorespiratory fitness by having them "listen" to their heartbeat by placing their hands on chest, first while at rest and then following exercise. Introduce the class to pulse rate and the counting of pulse on the carotid artery. Engage the class in tasks that demonstrate low to moderate to vigorous physical activity (e.g., stretching, jogging, walking, jumping rope, dribbling a ball in self-space). After each activity, have the children listen to their heartbeat and feel their pulse. Lead the class in a discussion of changes that take place in the body during vigorous physical activity (e.g., rapid heartbeat, sweating, heavy breathing).

Criteria for Assessment:
a. Recognizes that changes in heart rate occur as a result of participation in moderate to vigorous activity
b. Correctly identifies several physiological changes that occur at moderate or vigorous activity

3. Student journal

Following a discussion of muscular strength and endurance appropriate for second graders and participation in different activities that focus on climbing, hanging, and taking weight momentarily on hands, have the children write in their journals about their strength in climbing, hanging, and taking weight on hands. Assist each child in setting a goal for themselves (e.g., support weight on hanging rope, go half-way across the horizontal ladder, take weight on hands for a 3-second count).

Have the children illustrate their journal entries with a drawing of themselves. Ask them to circle the body parts (muscles) used for hanging, climbing, and supporting weight on hands.

Criteria for Assessment:
a. Establishes appropriate goal relative to muscular strength and endurance
b. Correctly identifies the body parts involved in hanging, climbing, and taking weight

on hands

4. Informal testing - observational record

Introduce the children to flexibility as a fitness component through the use of appropriate exercises or flexibility tasks, (e.g., stretching toward the toes while in the sit-and-reach position, the trunk lift, and the finger touch behind the back [shoulder stretch]). Lead discussions of specificity as students become aware of flexibility in some areas and lack of flexibility in others. Record the names of students experiencing difficulty in satisfactorily completing the various flexibility tasks.

Criteria for Assessment:
a. Touches toes while seated in the proper sit-and-reach position
b. Successfully completes the upper trunk lift
c. Touches fingers while performing the shoulder stretch
d. Correctly associates these activities with the component of flexibility

5. Demonstrates responsible personal and social behavior in physical activity settings.

Second graders know safe practices, physical education class rules and procedures, and are able to apply them with little or no reinforcement. They practice cooperation by successfully working with a partner and in small groups to accomplish an assigned task.

The emphasis for the second grade student will be to:

- Apply rules, procedures, and safe practices with little or no reinforcement.

- Follow directions.

- Work cooperatively with another to complete an assigned task.

Sample Benchmarks:

1. Uses equipment and space safely and properly.
2. Responds positively to an occasional reminder about a rule infraction.
3. Practices specific skills as assigned until the teacher signals the end of practice.
4. Stops activity immediately at the signal to do so.
5. Honestly reports the results of work.
6. Invites a peer to take his or her turn at a piece of apparatus before repeating a turn.
7. Assists partner by sharing observations about skill performance during practice.

Assessment Examples:

1. Self-assessment

After a partner task, the students are requested to list at least two things they did to be a good partner in the activity and one thing they could have done better to help their partner.

Criteria for Assessment:
a. Completes the assignment as directed
b. Responses identify "good" partner behavior
c. Responses accurately describe their own behavior

2. Student project

Students are asked to create during art class a picture book of rules and procedures for physical education that are to be done during art class. The class as a whole identifies and creates a comprehensive and accurate list of important rules and procedures. Each student writes down the rule or procedure they would like to draw. The teacher approves and assigns each student a rule or procedure.

Criteria for Assessment:
a. Accurately interprets the selected or assigned rule
b. Completes assignment with an obvious effort

3. Teacher observation - observational record

Students are videotaped while working on gymnastics equipment. Student performance is judged according to whether they have worked productively, safely, and cooperatively with others. The teacher records the extent to which each of the criteria are met by the class as well as by each student. (Recording incidents of noncompliance in most cases will be the most efficient way to record this information.) The teacher shares the assessment results with the student to develop an awareness of undesirable behavior and assist in making improvements.

Criteria for Assessment:
a. Works on assigned task in a productive manner
b. Works safely (no crashes and with an awareness of each other)
c. Exhibits cooperative behaviors (taking turns, supportive comments, assisting each other with moving equipment)

4. Parental report

Students are given the assignment to select and practice at home several movement skills (e.g., balancing on one foot, catching a tossed ball) on which they need additional work. They must record what they did and for how long, and have their parents sign the record at the end of the week.

Criteria for Assessment:

a. Identifies correctly the skills needing additional work
b. Practices identified skill at least three times a week for 15 minutes
c. Records performance accurately and neatly

5. Peer assessment

Students are given a task of practicing the underhand throw at a target with a partner. Students may choose the type and size of ball, distance from the target (enough distance to produce a throw and not a toss), and the height of the target. Partners assist each other by marking a score sheet for accuracy for each of five throws. Partners change roles after five throws. Take as many turns as the time allows.

Criteria for Assessment:
a. Chooses appropriate ball and placement of target for personal competence
b. Records partner's performance accurately and honestly
c. Assists partner by speaking politely and taking turns
d. Assumes personal responsibility for the results of the activity

6. Demonstrates understanding and respect for differences among people in physical activity settings

The focus in the primary grades is building a foundation for successful interpersonal communication during group activity. Emphasis is placed on identifying concepts such as cooperation, sharing, and consideration regardless of differences. Improving motor skills gives children a basis and appreciation for working with others in cooperative movement, sharing, and/or working together to solve a problem or tackle a challenge.

The emphasis for the second grade student will be to:

• Play and cooperate with others regardless of personal differences (e.g., gender, ethnicity, disability).

• Treat others with respect during play.

• Resolve conflicts in socially acceptable ways.

Sample Benchmarks:

1. Appreciates the benefits that accompany cooperation and sharing.
2. Displays consideration of others in physical activity settings.
3. Demonstrates the elements of socially acceptable conflict resolution.

Assessment Examples:

1.   Oral test - observational record

Teacher prepares a set of pictures that illustrate cooperative and sharing activities and noncooperative and nonsharing activities. Alternatively, the teacher could provide demonstrations of various activities. Students are asked to identify the illustrated activity as sharing, cooperative, nonsharing, or noncooperative. For non-sharing and non-cooperative pictures, students identify how they would change the behavior to make it more cooperative or sharing.

Criteria for Assessment:
a. Correctly identifies activities that involve sharing and cooperation
b. Offers ways to make games and activities more cooperative
c. Demonstrates awareness of personal behavior and the role that it played in past activities with regard to cooperation and sharing

2. Role playing - observational record

Students are asked to create a play dealing with conflict resolution during physical activity.

Criteria for Assessment:
a. Identifies action leading to the conflict
b. Identifies consequences of the conflict
c. Identifies alternative and socially acceptable methods for resolving the conflict

3. Interview - observational record

Following a game, the students are asked to demonstrate or verbalize examples of cooperation and sharing that occurred during the activity.

Criteria for Assessment:
a. Cites several examples of cooperation and sharing
b. Identifies ways in which all students were included
c. Recognizes the new friendships formed as the result of game play

7. Understands that physical activity provides the opportunity for enjoyment, challenge, self-expression, and social interaction.

As second graders, students are beginning to function as members of a group. They can work cooperatively with a partner for brief periods of time. Enjoyment comes from a growing competence of movement skills as they begin to master selected skills such as skipping, hopping, galloping, and running. Trying new activities provides challenge. They are beginning to express their feelings through their activity as well as identify activities they like and dislike.

The emphasis for the second grade student will be to:

• Gain competence to provide increased enjoyment in movement.

• Try new activities.

• Express feelings about and during physical activity.

• Enjoy interaction with friends through physical activity.

Sample Benchmarks:

1. Appreciates the benefits that accompany cooperation and sharing
2. Accepts the feelings resulting from challenges, successes, and failures in physical activity
3. Willingly tries new activities

Assessment Examples:

1. Event task - observational record

Students are asked to express a variety of feelings (e.g., happiness, sadness, anger, frustration, joy) during a creative movement or dance lesson through the use of a variety of shapes, postures, and movements. Students are asked to discuss with the class situations in physical activity that bring about these feelings.

Criteria for Assessment:
a. Uses movement to communicate feelings
b. Verbally expresses feelings that result from participation in physical activities

2. Group project

Working as a class, students shall design an obstacle course of straight, curved, and zigzag pathways using wands, ropes and other suitable manipulative materials. Each pathway designed must connect with another pathway. After completion of the obstacle course, students will decide what locomotor movements to use in traveling the various pathways.

Criteria for Assessment:
a. Shares equipment with others when building the obstacle course
b. Cooperates with others in determining pathways and locomotor movements

3. Student journal

At different times throughout the year, students are request to write and/or draw in their journals:

* How they felt when they scored a goal, made a basket, or kicked a ball really far.
* How they felt when they missed the ball for the kick or the hit.
* How they felt when the class tried an activity for the first time.
* Their favorite activities in physical education class.

Criteria for Assessment:
a. Identifies feelings associated with successes and failures
b. Expresses these feelings in their journal

4. Teacher observation - observational record

Students are observed periodically during physical activity, checking for non-verbal signs of enjoyment, positive interaction with others, and willingness to try new activities.

Criteria for Assessment:
a. Participates willingly in new activities
b. Continues to participate when not successful on the first try
c. Cooperates with others during physical education activities

Fourth Grade

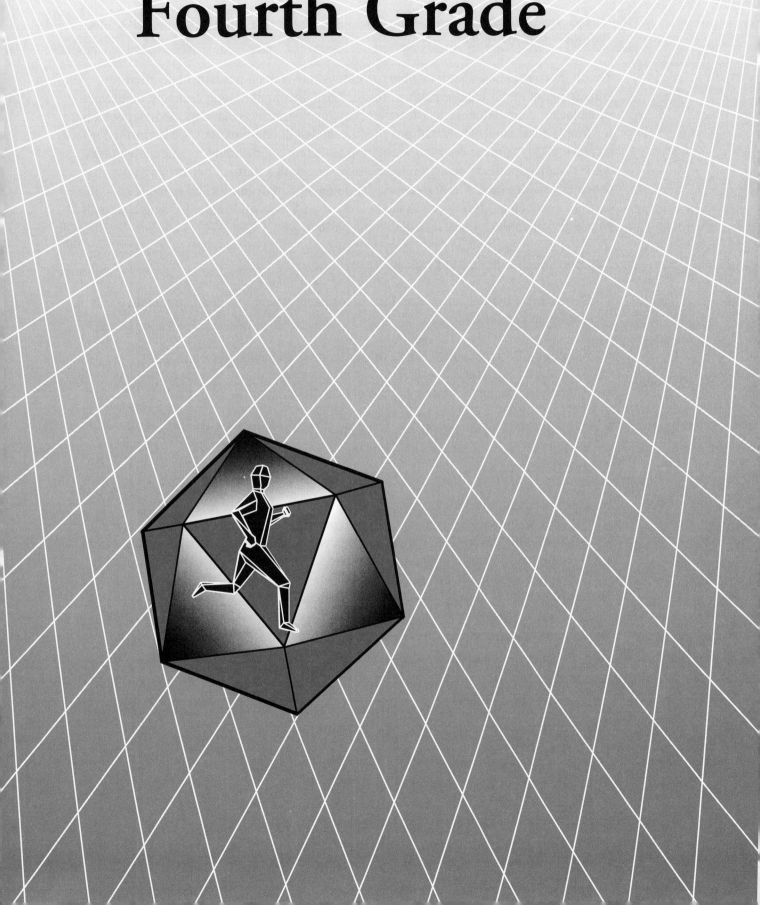

Fourth Grade

> **1. Demonstrates competency in many movement forms and proficiency in a few movement forms.**

Fourth grade students should be able to demonstrate refined fundamental patterns. Attainment of mature motor patterns for the basic locomotor, nonlocomotor, and selected isolated manipulative skills (throwing, catching, striking) is an expected exit outcome for fourth grade students. Variations of skills and skill combinations are performed in increasingly dynamic and complex environments (e.g., performing manipulative tasks while dodging, performing a gymnastics sequence with a partner, performing a formal dance to music). In addition, students should be able to acquire some specialized skills basic to a movement form (i.e., basketball chest pass, soccer dribble, fielding a softball with a glove) and to use those skills with a partner.

The emphasis for the fourth grade student will be to:

- Demonstrate mature form in all locomotor patterns and selected manipulative and nonlocomotor skills.

- Adapt a skill to the demands of a dynamic, unpredictable environment.

- Acquire beginning skills of a few specialized movement forms.

- Combine movement skills in applied settings.

Sample Benchmarks:

1. Throws, catches, and kicks using mature form.
2. Dribbles and passes a basketball to a moving receiver.
3. Balances with control on a variety of objects (balance board, large apparatus, skates)
4. Develops and refines a gymnastics sequence demonstrating smooth transitions.
5. Develops and refines a creative dance sequence into a repeatable pattern.
6. Jumps and lands for height/distance using mature form.

Assessment Examples:

1. Teacher observation - observational record

Students are asked to receive and send a basketball pass to a partner on the move. The teacher observes the passing and uses a checklist to annotate the performance.

Criteria for Assessment:
a. Receives the pass and sends it in one motion
b. Passes ahead of the moving player (receiver does not have to stop)
c. Receiving student cuts into a space to receive the pass

2. Event task - observational record

Students are asked to combine a balance, a roll, and a traveling action into a gymnastics sequence. The sequence must include all the components and a clear beginning and ending.

Criteria for Assessment:
a. Exhibits a balance, a role, and a traveling action during the performance
b. Demonstrates a clear beginning and ending to the sequence
c. Demonstrates smooth transitions between the various skills

3. Peer observation

Have partners observe the preparatory phase of a designated skill in an attempt to ascertain the correct use of critical elements. For example, student A will throw a ball toward a target five times using the overhand pattern while student B observes the performance, focusing on a single critical element during the preparatory phase (e.g., opposite foot forward, side to target, arm pulled way back). The observing student gives a "thumbs up" if the critical element is correct; if incorrect, the observing student tells what is needed to improve the movement.

Criteria for Assessment:
a. Thrower displays the critical element that is the focus of the observation
b. Observer makes an accurate judgment on the performance

2. Applies movement concepts and principles to the learning and development of motor skills.

The fourth grade student should be able to use critical elements to refine personal performance of fundamental and selected specialized motor skills, as well as to provide feedback to others. They should be able to identify and apply concepts that impact the quality of movement performance in increasingly complex movement situations. For example, a ball must be passed in front of a moving player, appropriate practice improves performance, and the lower the center of gravity the more stable an object.

The emphasis for the fourth grade student will be to:

• Apply critical elements to improve personal performance in fundamental and selected specialized motor skills.

• Use critical elements of fundamental and specialized movement skills to provide feedback to others.

• Recognize and apply concepts that impact the quality of increasingly complex movement performance.

Sample Benchmarks:

1. Transfers weight from feet to hands at fast and slow speeds using large extensions (e.g., mule kick, handstand, cartwheel).
2. Accurately recognizes the critical elements of a throw made by a fellow student and provides feedback to that student.
3. Consistently strikes a softly thrown ball with a bat or paddle demonstrating an appropriate grip.
4. Understands that appropriate practice improves performance.

Assessment Examples:

1. Teacher observation - observational record

After initial practice of a skill the teacher gives students a cue to improve performance. The teacher records the names of those students who are having difficulty practicing with an intent to use the information given to them.

 Criteria for Assessment:
a. Practice shows a definite intent to use the information given to them to improve performance.
b. Stays with the focus given by the teacher until that aspect of performance is not a problem.

2. Student log

Students record in a log or journal the results of a specific skill (e.g., number of shots made) during a 10 minute daily practice period for two weeks. At the end of the designated time period (i.e., two weeks) the data from the log is used to develop a learning curve on a graph. On the horizontal axis, students plot the days and on the vertical axis plot the scores (number of successful shots). Students apply data to the graph and connect the entries to show the overall learning trend. Students then analyze the information shown on the graph to determine the progress over time.

Criteria for Assessment:
a. Maintains log correctly.
b. Appropriately prepare graph from log information
c. Correctly assesses progress as a result of practice

3. Event task

Students are requested to design a game of throwing and catching for one or two persons to play. The game must include the underhand throwing skill that has been taught in class. Students write a description of the game so students in another class could, after reading the information, play the game. They are also asked to describe how the

critical elements of the skill might change when used in different conditions.
Criteria for Assessment:
a. Game incorporates use of underhand throwing and catching skills
b. Description of game adequately identifies needed skills and critical elements of each
c. Description accurately describes how critical elements might change under varying conditions

4. Peer observation

Students observe a classmate in a performance (live or videotaped) showing combinations of various basic skills used in a changing environment. The observer analyzes the skills performed for maturity of movement by determining the critical elements used or missing. For each skill combination, students must first identify if the performance represents a mature pattern. If the performance has critical elements missing, students must identify those missing elements. Finally, they should suggest ideas for either practice or use of available cues to improve performance.

Criteria for Assessment:
a. Accurately identifies the critical elements required of the various movement skills
b. Recognizes the presence or absence of critical elements during performance
c. Suggests appropriate practice activities

5. Written test

Students are given a written test in which they are asked to describe the difference in catching a ball at a high level and catching a ball at a low level. Moreover, they should describe (a) which critical elements are the same, (b) which are different, and (c) what information is available from the thrower to inform the catcher as to the height of the ball.

Criteria for Assessment:
a. Correctly identifies critical elements and similarities/differences of catching at a high or low level.
b. Correctly identifies characteristics of the throw that predict the height of the thrown ball.

3. Exhibits a physically active lifestyle.

The intent of this standard is the beginning development of an awareness of participation in physical activity as a conscious decision and personal choice for both enjoyment and health-related benefits. Students at this age will begin to be aware of those activities they enjoy, and will participate in activity to improve their own personal skill and enjoyment and should be encouraged to do so. This knowledge should be connected with their personal decisions for participation outside of physical education class. Students should also be able to describe personal, psychological and emotional benefits of their participation in physical activity.

The emphasis for the fourth grade student will be to:

- Select and participate regularly in physical activities for the purpose of improving skill and health.

- Identify the benefits derived from regular physical activity.

- Identify several moderate to vigorous physical activities that provide personal pleasure.

Sample Benchmarks:

1. Regularly participates in physical activity for the purpose of developing a healthy lifestyle.
2. Describes healthful benefits that result from regular and appropriate participation in physical activity.
3. Identifies at least one activity that they participate in on a regular basis (formal or informal.)
4. Is beginning to be aware of opportunities for more formal participation in physical activities in the community.

Assessment Examples:

1. Student log

During daily recess, select from a variety of health-enhancing physical activities. Participate in each activity for at least 15 minutes four to five times per week for one month. Keep a log of the date of the participation, the activity selected, the health-related objective, and comments about how you felt during the activity. At the end of the month, write a letter to your parents describing the activity and how you feel after having completed the activity.

Criteria for Assessment:
a. Selects an activity that is appropriate to the objective
b. Sustains activity throughout the time period
c. Writes accurate and complete letters to parents

2. Written test

Students are asked to identify each component of fitness and to describe both an exercise and an activity that has the potential to develop that component.

Criteria for Assessment:
a. Accurately identifies each component

b. Correctly identifies appropriate exercise for each component
c. Correctly identifies appropriate activity for each component.

4. Group project - observational record

Use the information from each student's physical activity log to make a wall chart showing favorite activities of all students in the class. Discuss differences and similarities in the potential of each activity to contribute to health-related fitness and possible reasons for those differences.

Criteria for Assessment:
a. Identifies correctly those activities that contribute to different components of health-related fitness
b. Shows awareness of the individual preferences for different activities

4. Achieves and maintains a health-enhancing level of physical fitness.

By the fourth grade, students will begin to match different types of physical activity with underlying physical fitness components and should participate in moderate to vigorous physical activities in a variety of settings. Students should begin to be able to interpret the results and understand the significance of information provided by formal measures of physical fitness. Fitness testing may be introduced at this level. Meeting the criterion health standards prescribed by Fitnessgram is desirable.

The emphasis for the fourth grade student will be to:

* Identify several activities related to each component of physical fitness.

* Associate results of fitness testing to personal health status and ability to perform various activities.

* Meet the health-related fitness standards as defined by Fitnessgram.

Sample Benchmarks:

1. Engages in appropriate activity that results in the development of muscular strength.
2. Maintains continuous aerobic activity for a specified time and/or activity.
3. Supports, lifts, and controls body weight in a variety of activities.
4. Regularly participates in physical activity for the purpose of improving physical fitness.

Assessment Examples:

1. Student project

Have the students collect pictures of people participating in physical activities and identify those activities that contribute to each component of health-related fitness.

Criteria for Assessment:
a. Provides a minimum of two examples for each fitness component
b. Associates activity with appropriate component of fitness.

2. Student Log

Students record their after-school activities for one week. Ask them to indicate the activities that are vigorous in nature and identify the fitness components related to the different activities. Parent or guardian is to sign the log each day.

Criteria for Assessment:
a. Accurately records after-school activities
b. Identifies appropriate fitness component related to each activity
c. Parents or guardian sign the log

3. Student project

Students are ask to select an exercise intended to achieve a personal fitness-related goal. Practice the exercise regularly over the course of several weeks (specify the exact length of time). Have the student record the results of each exercise session and graph the progress. For example, the student's goal may be to increase muscular endurance of the abdominal muscles through sit-ups. Initially they may be capable of one set of 8 sit-ups and should be able to do considerably more at the end of the month. Progress should be graphed.

Criteria for Assessment:
a. Correctly identifies a personal goal that needs work
b. Records progress towards goal on a regular basis
c. Shows consistent improvement over time
d. Meets their own goal at the end of the month

4. Student journal

Following a fall health and fitness screening (informal testing) have students identify their strengths and weaknesses based on test results. Students write their personal fitness goals for the year and what they would like to do to work toward those goals.

Criteria for Assessment:
a. Accurately identifies their strengths and weaknesses
b. Establishes realistic personal fitness goals
c. Makes appropriate decisions about working toward the stated goals

5. Formal testing

The student participates in the Fitnessgram Physical Fitness Test and meets the criteria established for their age and gender.

5. Demonstrates responsible personal and social behavior in physical activity settings.

Students identify the purposes for and follow, with few reminders, activity-specific safe practices, rules, procedures, and etiquette. They continue to develop cooperation skills to enable completion of a common goal while working with a partner or in small groups. They can work independently and productively for short periods of time.

The emphasis for the fourth grade student will be to:

- Follow, with few reminders, activity-specific rules, procedures, and etiquette.

- Utilize safety principles in activity situations.

- Work cooperatively and productively with a partner or small group.

- Work independently and on-task for short periods of time.

Sample Benchmarks:

1. When given the opportunity, arranges gymnastics equipment safely in a manner appropriate to the task.
2. Takes seriously their role to teach an activity or skill to two other classmates.
3. Works productively with a partner to improve the overhand throw pattern for distance by using the critical elements of the process.
4. Accepts the teacher's decision regarding a personal rule infraction without displaying negative reactions toward others.
5. Assesses their own performance problems without blaming others.

Assessment Examples:

1. Teacher observation - observational record

The teacher monitors on-task and off-task activity for each student several times during a unit and records the extent of on-task activity. Each student is observed at least once in four intervals of one minute set aside for this purpose.

Criteria for Assessment:
a. Demonstrates on-task activity 90% of the time

2. Event task - observational record

Students are divided into groups of three or four in order to work on pitching, batting, and catching a whiffle ball. Following an explanation of the importance of getting equipment set up, giving every member of the group an opportunity to practice each skill, and working to help each other get better at the various skills, students are given the opportunity to practice the skills for a specified length of time.

Criteria for Assessment:
a. The group moves quickly to get organized and starts practice within a short time of the signal to begin.
b. Each member of the group gets about the same amount of practice on each skill.
c. Members of each group work to help one another get better at the skills involved.
d. The group stays focused and on-task for the time allocated for the practice.

3. Teacher observation - observational record

Several days into a unit, students are ask to identify the aspects of a skill or fitness component on which they feel that they need additional work. The teacher suggests that the first 5 minutes of the next class period will be time assigned for each individual to work on that skill or fitness component. Student must write down what it is they want to work on and how they are going to work on it.

Criteria for Assessment:
a. Accurately identifies what skill or fitness component needs remediation
b. Selects an appropriate way to work on the skill or fitness component
c. Pursues work on the identified skill or fitness component for at least 5 minutes

4. Group project

Students create an activity wall chart comparing differences of safety practices, rules, procedures, and etiquette for each activity presented in class during the course of the year.

Criteria for Assessment:
a. Identifies appropriate safety practices, rules, etc. for the chosen activities
a. Recognizes similarities and differences among activities

6. Demonstrates understanding and respect for differences among people in physical activity settings

Building on the foundation laid in the early grades, fourth grade students are encouraged to develop a cultural/ethnic self-awareness. Recognizing and appreciating one's own heritage lays the groundwork for understanding and appreciating the differences in others. Activities such as dance/music; creative games; and games from varied cultures, ethnic groups, and countries provide an excellent medium for encouraging students to explore their cultural/ethnic heritage.

The emphasis for the fourth grade student will be to:

- Explore cultural/ethnic self-awareness through participation in physical activity.

- Recognize the attributes that individuals with differences can bring to group activities.

- Experience differences and similarities among people of different backgrounds by participating in activities of national, cultural, and ethnic origins.

Sample Benchmarks:

1. Recognizes differences and similarities in others' physical activity.
2. Indicates respect for persons from different backgrounds and the cultural significance they attribute to various games, dances, and physical activities.
3. Demonstrates acceptance of the skills and abilities of others through verbal and nonverbal behavior.

Assessment Examples:

1. Student project

Students are asked to focus on "discovering their roots" as they present a game, dance, or other physical activity associated with their origins. The project can include reading activities and interviews with parents and relatives to discover cultural/ethnic roots; written or art expressions of associated physical activities; and a performance/demonstration of selected physical activities complete with costumes, equipment, and music.

Criteria for Assessment:
a. Demonstrates a knowledge of his/her cultural/ethnic roots.
b. Describes how the selected activity relates to the environment in which it was practiced (e.g., climate, geography, historical tradition).
c. Looks for similarities and differences between selected physical activities and activities popular today.

2. Event task

The following are some suggested student activities for possible event tasks related to developing an awareness of the strengths and limitations of the physically challenged:

- Play wheelchair basketball. Write about it afterwards. Describe your feelings and frustrations.
- Create a game in which a person who is blind would be able to compete equally with a sighted person. Describe the challenges you encountered while developing this game.
- Create a dance that a person with a hearing disability could perform. Describe the challenges you encountered while developing this game.

Criteria for Assessment:
a. Completes the required task
b. Demonstrates an understanding of the similarities and differences of persons with disabilities

c. Recognizes strengths of each participant

3. Portfolio

Working in a group of three or four members, students will chose a country of inte est and a dance native to that country. Students will learn the dance and teach it to other members of the class. Each group will examine all dances presented for sim larities and differences and attempt to determine reasons for similarities and diffe ences. A portfolio consisting of a description of the country and why it was chosen, the selected dance and why it was chosen, and interpretive descriptions of the sim larities and differences of the various dances presented in class will be submitted by each group.

Criteria for Assessment:
a. Willingly participates in learning games, dances, and activities from other parts of the world
b. Accepts lessons in a positive manner
c. Recognizes similarities and differences between dances from different countries
d. Identifies reasons for the similarities and differences among dances of various countries

> **7. Understands that physical activity provides the opportunity for enjoy-ment, challenge, self-expression, and social interaction.**

Fourth graders can identify activities that they consider to be fun. Enjoyment is directly related to competence in a particular activity. They are challenged by learning a new physical activity and enjoy broadening their repertoire of move-ment skills. Success and improvement are attributed to effort and practice. They tend to choose an appropriate level of challenge in an activity so as to experience success and engage in activity with students of similar skill levels.

The emphasis for the fourth grade student will be to:

• Experience enjoyment while participating in physical activity.

• Enjoy practicing activities to increase skill competence.

• Interact with friends while participating in group activities.

• Use physical activity as a means of self-expression.

Sample Benchmarks:

1. Experience positive feelings as a result of involvement in physical activity.
2. Design games, gymnastics, and dance sequences that are personally interest-ing.
3. Celebrate personal successes and achievements as well as those of others.

Assessment Examples:

1. Class project

Students are asked to create a mural entitled, "Favorite Activities in Physical Education", using butcher paper that is then placed around the gym walls. (Invite classroom teachers, administrators, and parents to see the children's' work.)

Criteria for Assessment:
a. Willingly participates in the class project
b. Art work shows enjoyment of activity

2. Student log

Students select a goal from options provided by the teacher (e.g., walking a certain distance, jumping rope a number of minutes) that requires the group to work together to achieve the goal. While working to achieve the goal, each student is asked to keep a log of individual as well as group progress towards the goal.

Criteria for Assessment
a. Contributes as a participating member of the group
b. Demonstrates an understanding of individual and group successes through log comments

3. Student project

Students will work with the teacher to set a personal physical activity goal, such as completing the one-mile run, achieving a particular gymnastics or games/sports skill. Upon achievement of the goal, students are asked to describe their feelings after "climbing the seemingly insurmountable hill."

Criteria for Assessment:
a. Expresses personal satisfaction in his or her accomplishment
b. Expresses appreciation for the success of others
c. Shares feelings with others in the class

4. Portfolio

Students are requested to develop a portfolio illustrating games, gymnastics, or dances in which they frequently participate. Students shall then select their favorite activity in the portfolio and write a paragraph telling why this is their favorite. Ask them to share their portfolio with the class and describe their favorite activity and why they like it.

Criteria for Assessment:

a. Selects activities that are personally interesting and rewarding

b. Explains why they have selected a particular activity as their favorite

c. Willingly shares their portfolio and favorite activity with the class

Sixth Grade

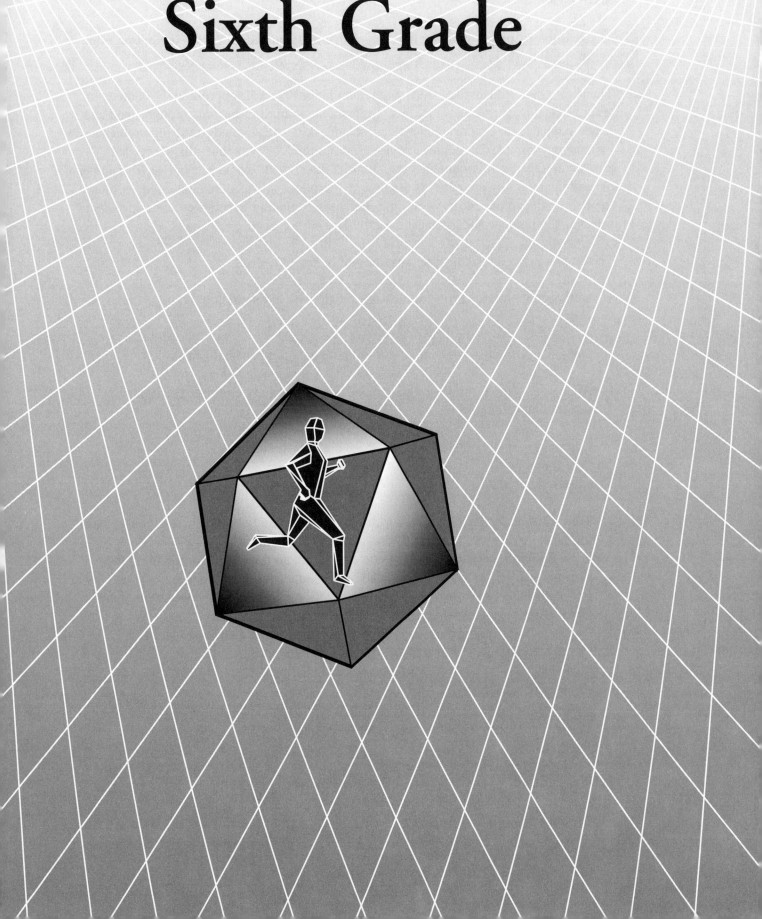

Sixth Grade

1. Demonstrates competency in many movement forms and proficiency in a few movement forms.

The sixth grade student uses skills and combinations of skills appropriately in the context of actual performance situations. Stunts and gymnastics become more refined and dance sequences are more sophisticated. Game skills are adapted to the requirements of increasingly complex strategies and are used in more complex, but still, somewhat unstructured game environments (e.g., limited rules, modified equipment, small numbers of participants). Mature patterns are now expected for all basic manipulative, locomotor, and nonlocomotor skills, while the student is beginning to acquire the basic skills of selected sport, dance and gymnastics activities.

The emphasis for the sixth grade student will be to:

- Demonstrate mature form for all basic manipulative, locomotor and nonlocomotor skills.

- Demonstrate increasing competence in more advanced specialized skills.

- Adapt and combine skills to the demands of increasingly complex situations of selected movement forms.

- Demonstrate beginning strategies for net and invasion games.

Sample Benchmarks:

1. Throws a variety of objects demonstrating both accuracy and force (e.g., basketball, footballs, frisbees).
2. Hand dribbles and foot dribbles while preventing an opponent from stealing the ball.
3. Designs and performs gymnastics and dance sequences that combine traveling, rolling, balancing, and weight transfer into smooth flowing sequences with intentional changes in direction, speed and flow.
4. Keeps an object going continuously with a partner using a striking pattern.
5. Places the ball away from an opponent in a racket sport activity.

Assessment Examples:

1. Teacher observation - observational record

Students are asked to perform basic dribbling and passing skills used in soccer while working with a partner in an attempt to score against an opponent.

Criteria for Assessment:
a. Passes when the defense attacks, maintains the ball when the defense holds back

b. Executes accurate passes ahead of the receiver

c. Receiver moves into a space to create a passing angle not covered by the defense

d. Both players receive the ball in such a way as to set up a continuous dribble or pass

2. Self-assessment - checklist

Following a period of working on throwing different types of objects (frisbees, footballs, deck tennis rings) students are asked to identify the number of different objects they have thrown and the type of throwing patterns they have used with these objects. They are also asked to do a self-assessment of their throwing performance using a checklist provided by the teacher.

Criteria for Assessment:

a. Recognizes differences in various types of throws

b. Compares and contrasts throwing of different objects for different purposes

c. Analyzes personal throwing skills accurately

3. Student project

Students are placed in groups of five or six members and are asked to role play the following scenario: The City Little League coach has asked your group to serve as assistant coaches this season. Specifically, the coach wants you to do a presentation of either (a) throwing a ball for varying distance OR (b) striking with a bat for a bunt versus a home run. Within each group, students should prepare a presentation to include an oral presentation of the various skills, explaining the variations of each, and a demonstration of the skills. Each person within the group must be part of the presentation. Each group will present their mini-demonstrations to the class.

Criteria for Assessment:

a. Demonstrates skills correctly

b. Compares and or contrasts variations within skills

c. Presentation is organized and interesting

4. Event task - observational record

As the final project in gymnastics, students are to design a 90-second routine for either mats or apparatus. They may choose to work alone or with a partner; the partner relationship may be mirror or side-by-side. The routine must include an approach, development, and ending shape or dismount. The development portion of the routine must include the following: a minimum of four balances of different shapes and bases of support, a minimum of three locomotor and/or nonlocomotor actions, weight transfers, and at least two inversions. The selection of music for the routine is a student decision. The routine is to be diagrammed or written on paper and practiced until the sequence is memorized in its entirety. The routine will be videotaped for inclusion in student portfolios.

Criteria for Assessment:

a. Routine includes all necessary components: approach, balances, weight transfers, inversion, dismount (ending shape)
b. Routine matches music in length
c. Demonstrates changes in tempo in routine
d. Selects balances and weight transfers that can be correctly performed (i.e., skills matched to personal gymnastic ability)
e. Maintains stillness in balances
f. Displays creativity in routine design
g. Transitions between movement are smooth

2. Applies movement concepts and principles to the learning and development of motor skills.

The sixth grade student is able to use and apply concepts from a variety of sources to enhance learning and performance. Specifically, this student should be able to begin to identify principles of practice and conditioning that enhance movement performance. They should be able to recognize similarities and differences between movement skills that use similar patterns and transfer appropriate concepts from one to the other. Students should be able to use information from a variety of sources (internal and external) to guide and improve performance. This student should be able to recognize and use basic offensive and defensive strategies.

The emphasis for the sixth grade student will be to:

*   Use information from a variety of sources of internal and external origin to improve performance.

*   Identify and apply principles of practice and conditioning that enhance performance.

*   Recognize general characteristics of movement that can be applied to specific settings (e.g., similarity of the ready position in striking movement forms).

*   Use basis offensive and defensive strategies in noncomplex settings.

Sample Benchmarks:

1. Detects, analyzes and corrects errors in personal movement patterns.
2. Identifies proper warm-up and cool-down techniques and the reasons for using them.
3. Identifies basic practice and conditioning principles that enhance performance.

Assessment Examples:

1. Student report

Partners videotape each other while striking a ball resting on a batting tee (five times) and while striking a ball thrown by a pitcher (five times). They review the tape with their partner and self-assess according to criteria presented to them in class. Based on this information they write a description of one or more of the following: the critical elements of batting; the consistency of their movement patterns; the differences in cues available when striking from a tee (closed skill) versus striking a pitched ball (open skill); and practice suggestions for improvement in each skill.

Criteria for Assessment:
a. Accurately describes the criteria for good batting
b. Accurately assesses their own consistency of performance
c. Accurately identifies cues available in open or closed skills
d. Selects appropriate practice options based on the differences between the two skills

2. Group Project

Students are asked to identify three basic offensive strategies and three basis defensive strategies from their two-on-two basketball games. These are discussed as a class and turned into the teacher at the end of the class period for evaluation.

Criteria for Assessment:
a. Correctly identifies three offensive and defensive strategies.
b. Identifies all the basic strategies.

3. Student journal

Students are ask to perform a self-assessment of their progress in throwing different types of objects (e.g., Frisbee, football, softball, deck tennis rings) and record this information in their journal. Moreover, they should describe the differences and similarities in throwing these objects and discuss which objects were easy/difficult to throw.

Criteria for Assessment:
a. Correctly identifies personal status on the use of critical elements of throwing.
b. Identifies differences and similarities that occur when applying principles of throwing to different objects.
c. Describes which objects they found easy/difficult to throw.

4. Student project

Students are requested to select an activity in which they are currently involved or one in which they would like to be involved and analyze the health-related fitness and motor fitness components that most affect performance. In addition, students should identify which components of fitness might be enhanced by participation in this activity. The analysis should also include a description of specific exercises that might be included in an adequate warm-up routine, conditioning program, and cool-down routine that will support the learning, mastery and performance of the selected activity.

Criteria for Assessment:
a. Correctly identifies the health-related fitness and motor fitness components that most effect performance in the selected activity
b. Correctly identifies components of fitness that would be enhanced by participation in the selected activity
c. Selects appropriate exercises that enhance the learning and performance of the selected activity

3. Exhibits a physically active lifestyle.

The intent of this standard for the sixth grade is the development of voluntary participation in out-of-class physical activities with the goal of developing interest and improving and maintaining an active lifestyle.. Physical activity choices are based on personal interests and capabilities, perceived social and physical benefits, challenge and enjoyment. As students gain more control over the decisions affecting their everyday living, the notion of a broad perspective of active and healthy lifestyle should be introduced.

The emphasis for the sixth grade student will be to:

* Identify opportunities in the school and community for regular participation in physical activity.

* Participate daily in some form of health-enhancing physical activity.

* Analyze personal interests and capabilities in regard to one's exercise behavior.

* Identify the critical aspects of a healthy lifestyle.

Sample Benchmarks:

1. Chooses to exercise at home for personal enjoyment and benefit.
2. Participates in games, sports, dance and outdoor pursuits both in and out of school based on individual interests and capabilities.
3. Identifies opportunities close to home for participation in different kinds of activities.

Assessment Examples:

1. Student project

Students are instructed to develop a chart that can be used to identify opportunities in the school and community for regular participation in physical activity. Various information can be included on the chart including the type of activity, the providing body, the address and phone number of the providing body, cost to participate, special equipment requirements, registration dates, and time of involvement. Students should be encouraged to gather the information and to organize their chart for ease of locating information about the various activities. Information can be summarized by creating a general class chart created from the information on the individual charts.

Criteria for Assessment:
a. Completes the chart relative to the number of community opportunities
b. Provides accurate information in the chart in terms of the amount and type of information provided for each activity
c. Organizes and presents ideas well

2. Student journal

The students are asked to keep a journal recording out-of-school physical activities in which they voluntarily engage in over a prescribed period of time. Physical activities that are required for life roles (e.g., survival, work, health-enhancing physical activity) should be included. Next to each activity the student should record how that activity can be performed in a more health-enhancing way (walking instead of riding; getting up to change the TV rather than using the remote). Students should describe the various factors in their lives that inhibit or enable them to participate regularly in health-enhancing physical activities and suggest ways in which they can change their daily routines to include more health-enhancing activity.

Criteria for Assessment:
a. Accurately completes the journal
b. Identifies factors inhibiting or promoting physical activity
c. Provides insightfulness regarding the modifications that could be made to daily routines

3. Portfolio

Students are asked to select a favorite physical activity. With teacher assistance, the student should set a goal for improvement of a skill for that activity and plan a 10 to 15 minute daily practice period. Furthermore, the student should keep a log of the actual practice that took place in accordance with the plan. In-class or out-of-class time may used to accomplish the task. Evidence of improvement is gathered and maintained in a portfolio that includes the log, established goals, rationale for selecting the activity and the goals, and any other evidence of participation in the activity.

Criteria for Assessment:
a. Selects appropriate goal
b. Develops appropriate plan
c. Meets goal
d. Presents project well

4. Achieves and maintains a health-enhancing level of physical fitness.

Sixth grade students should be able to participate in moderate to vigorous physical activities in a variety of settings for longer periods of time. In addition, students can assess their own heart rate, breathing rate, perceived exertion, and recovery rate during and following strenuous physical activity. Students are developing a better understanding of the components of fitness and how these relate to their overall fitness status. In conjunction with the teacher, students should be able to use information from fitness assessments to increase current levels of fitness on the various components and make progress toward desired goals:

The emphasis for the sixth grade student will be to:

- Participate in moderate to vigorous physical activity in a variety of settings.

- Monitor intensity of exercise.

- Begin to develop a strategy for the improvement of selected fitness components.

- Work somewhat independently with minimal supervision in pursuit of personal fitness goals.

- Meet the health-related fitness standards as defined by Fitnessgram.

Sample Benchmarks:

1. Keeps a record of heart rate before, during, and after vigorous physical activity.
2. Participates in fitness-enhancing organized physical activities outside of school (e.g., gymnastic clubs, community sponsored youth sports).
3. Engages in physical activity at the target heart rate for a minimum of 20 minutes.
4. Correctly demonstrates activities designed to improve and maintain muscular strength and endurance, flexibility, cardiorespiratory functioning, and proper body composition.

Assessment Examples:

1. Student journal

Students will record their heart rate before, during, and after engaging in five different types of physical activity, both sedentary and active, for a week (e.g., walking with parents, soccer practice, watching TV, raking leaves, riding a bike, physical education class). Students report in their journal the extent to which each of these activities has the potential to contribute to cardiorespiratory fitness.

Criteria for Assessment:

a. Accurately records heart rate before, during, and after activity
b. Accurately identifies the activities having the most value for cardiorespiratory fitness

2. Student log

Students maintain a log of the various kinds of physical activity they participate in for several weeks. The log should contain information regarding the duration of each exercise bout as well as frequency of participation.

Criteria for Assessment:
a. Participates in more than one type of moderate to vigorous physical activity outside of physical education class
b. Demonstrates vigorous activity for 20 minutes at least three times a week

3. Group project - observational record

Students, working in small groups, are asked to design a "fitness video" depicting exercises or activities appropriate for each component of health-related fitness. The group presentation will include a verbal description of each fitness component as well as demonstration of the selected exercises or physical activity. The group may choose a class presentation or an actual video.

Criteria for Assessment:
a. Presentation includes each of the health-related fitness components
b. Each student is actively involved in the exercise/activity demonstration
c. Physical activities are accurately matched to fitness components

4. Formal test

The student participates in the Fitnessgram Physical Fitness Test and meets the criteria established for their age and gender. Students failing to meet the recommended health standard will work with their teacher to set a goal, design, and implement a program of exercises and activities to address areas of need.

Criteria for Assessment:
a. Establishes realistic personal fitness goals
b. Selects appropriate activities to address area(s) of remediation
c. Participates regularly in the personal fitness program

5. Demonstrates responsible personal and social behavior in physical activity settings.

Sixth grade students identify the purposes for and participate in the establishment of safe practices, rules, procedures, and etiquette for specific activities. They develop cooperation skills to accomplish group or team goals in both cooperative and competi-

tive activities. Students are expected to work independently to complete assigned tasks.

The emphasis for the sixth grade student will be to:

* Participate in establishing rules, procedures, and etiquette that are safe and   effective for specific activity situations.

* Work cooperatively and productively in a group to accomplish a set goal in   both cooperative and competitive activities.

* Make conscious decisions about applying rules, procedures, and etiquette.

* Utilize time effectively to complete assigned tasks.

Sample Benchmarks:

1. Makes responsible decisions about using time, applying rules, and following through with the decisions made.
2. Uses time wisely when given the opportunity to practice and improve performance.
3. Makes suggestions for modifications in a game or activity that can improve the game.
4. Remains on-task in a group activity without close teacher monitoring.
5. Chooses a partner that he or she can work with productively.
6. Distinguishes between acts of "courage" and reckless acts.
7. Includes concerns for safety in self-designed activities.

Assessment Examples:

1. Event task - observational record

Students, working in groups of six to eight, create a list of characteristics that illustrate social responsibility. Students then design a game for all members of their group using their choice of equipment. The game must include the use of a striking pattern, with or without equipment, and have clear procedures for scoring and rule infractions. The teacher assesses the group interaction skills of members of the group and then asks students to identify a list of personal behaviors that make their group function well. Students then assess their own personal responsibilities while playing the game.

Criteria for Assessment:
a. Demonstrates a majority of the following group interaction behaviors as appropriate: listening; staying focused and on-task; helping others; proposing alternative solutions; conflict resolution; including and supporting all members of the group
b. Identifies several key ideas critical to making a group function well
c. Assumes responsibility for self

2. Teacher observation - observational record

Several students are observed each class period to assess the extent to which they are able to remain focused in an independent practice situation. A simple yes or no checklist or a more extensive rating scale may be used to facilitate this assessment.

Criteria for Assessment:
a. Maximizes practice opportunities
b. Displays little evidence of off-task behavior.
c. Eager to begin practice and reluctant to stop practicing
d. Demonstrates that effort is being made to "do it right"

3. Event task - observational record

Students, working in pairs, are given the opportunity to design and practice a gymnastics sequence using a combination of skills that they have learned during class. The students are instructed to choose skills at their own ability level and those they "can really polish." Students are told they will be evaluated on their choice of skills and their form, rather than on the level of difficulty of the skills they choose.

Criteria for Assessment:
a. Chooses skills of an appropriate difficulty level
b. Follows rules specific to the selected skill
c. Uses practice time appropriately
d. Shares practice space with others in the class

4. Teacher observation - observational record

The teacher is beginning a new unit on an activity in which students have had instruction in previous years. The teacher holds a class discussion to present safety rules and procedures for the class and to assess the degree to which students are able to anticipate, identify, and develop appropriate procedures to make the environment safe and maintain proper care of the equipment used.

Criteria for Assessment:
a. Identifies the critical dimensions of safety for the activity
b. Establishes rules and procedures that adequately address the potential safety problems of the activity

6. Demonstrates understanding and respect for differences among people in physical activity settings

By the sixth grade, students should be able to recognize the contribution of participation in physical activity to multicultural/ethnic awareness and the development of inclusionary behavior. They understand and respect the contributions of others with like and different skill levels to the group or team goal. Furthermore, they understand the cultural heritage of their own families and recognize that their classmates also have a cultural heritage that is important to them.

The emphasis for the sixth grade student will be to:

- Acknowledge differences in the behaviors of people of different gender, culture, ethnicity, and disability and seek to learn more about both similarities and differences.

- Cooperate with disabled peers and those of different gender, race, and ethnicity.

- Work cooperatively with both more and less skilled peers.

Sample Benchmarks:

1. Recognizes the role of games, sports, and dance in getting to know and understand others of like and different backgrounds.
2. Through verbal and nonverbal behavior demonstrates cooperation with peers of different gender, race, and ethnicity in a physical activity setting.
3. Seek out, participate with, and show respect for persons of like and different skill levels.
4. Recognizes the importance of one's personal heritage.

Assessment Examples:

1. Event task - observational record

Students in a group are asked to identify their personal strengths and weaknesses in respect to physical ability, as well as those of others in the group. They will design a game that will utilize these various skills. Students will be encouraged to switch positions. To switch positions, students must first determine the skills or expertise of the person in that position and then work with that person to become an "expert" for the position. Assessment can be made through teacher observation and oral or written expression.

Criteria for Assessment:
a. Helps to organize the team by placing everyone in their most advantageous position
b. Participates personally rather than delegating all activity to others
c. Recognizes their own strengths and weaknesses
d. Willingly uses their skills to help others
e. Understands, recognizes, and expresses orally or through written work that everyone can contribute to team performance

2. Student report

Recognizing that many of the games and sports played in the United States originated in other countries, students are asked to choose two sports that had origins in other countries. Students prepare a report that briefly describes the similarities and differences in how the sport was originally played and how it is played in this country.

Criteria for Assessment:
a. Identifies several differences and similarities in the way the selected game is

played in the native country and how it is played in the United States.
b. Describes the effects on the game of the cultures in both the country identified and in the United States

3. Role playing - observational record

Students are provided blindfolds and requested to play the role of persons with blindness (persons in wheelchairs or with deafness can also be simulated). The remaining students are divided into small groups and given the task of developing strategies for including the persons with blindness in a group activity. At the end of class, students who played the role of the individual with blindness and the other students are encouraged to discuss their experiences and come to a consensus regarding inclusion of persons with a disability in physical activity.

Criteria for Assessment:
a. Identifies strategies for including physically challenged individuals in physical activity
b. Identifies the challenges that a person with a disability is faced with when participating in physical activity

7. Understands that physical activity provides the opportunity for enjoyment, challenge, self-expression, and social interaction.

Sixth graders attach great importance to group membership; they will choose participation in physical activity to be with their peers. They can recognize and appreciate skilled performance in a variety of activities and choose to participate in those activities in which they experience success. Skill in sport and physical activity is valued as students respect those with high levels of ability. Physical activity can become an important avenue for self-expression for these students. Risk-taking, adventure, and competitive activities provide the opportunity for challenge, enjoyment, and positive social interaction.

The emphasis for the sixth grade student will be to:

- Recognize physical activity as a positive opportunity for social and group interaction.

- Demonstrate enjoyment from participation in physical activities.

- Recognize that success in physical activities leads to recognition from peers.

- Use physical activity to express feelings.

- Seek personally challenging experiences in physically active opportunities.

Sample Benchmarks:

1. Recognizes the role of games, sports, and dance in getting to know and

understand self and others.

2. Identifies benefits resulting from participation in different forms of physical activities.

3. Describes ways to use the body and movement activities to communicate ideas and feelings.

4. Seeks physical activity in informal settings that utilize skills and knowledge gained in physical education classes.

Assessment Examples:

1. Group project - observational record

Involve the class in an adventure/risk taking type activity. Following the activity, have the students describe emotions experienced during the activity. Ask the students how cooperation and communication were used during the activity, when these skills might be used during the activity, and when these skills might be needed in other physical activity settings.

Criteria for Assessment:
a. Cooperates and communicates with others during the adventure/risk taking activity
b. Shares emotions experienced during the activity
c. Recognizes common emotions experienced by self and others
d. Accepts feelings expressed by others and is capable of relating personal feelings to those expressed by others
e. Relates personal feelings to other situations

2. Student project

Students are asked to design a brochure for new students entering the school that outlines the various sport, gymnastics, and dance activities available, both inside and outside the school setting. The brochure should include an explanation of the nature of the activity and the benefits to the person as a result of participation.

Criteria for Assessment:
a. Identifies the various physical activities available
b. Explains the benefits resulting from participation in the various activities

3. Event task - observational record

Students, working alone, or with a partner or in a small group, shall create a "Colors of Emotions Dance." The students will, through movements and shapes, portray what the color represents to them, with the expressive movements progressing from the concrete to the abstract.

Criteria for Assessment:
a. Identifies the emotions associated with the color
b. Communicates ideas and feelings through the dance

4. Student project - journal

With teacher assistance, the students are requested to identify a goal they would like to accomplish as a result of experiences in physical education class (e.g., improving a skill, reaching a fitness goal, doing an adventure activity, participation in a sport, dance, recreational activity). Assist the students in creating a plan for meeting the goal, including participation in physical activity outside of physical education class (e.g., recreational leagues, intramurals, clubs). Students are asked to document in a journal their progress toward the goal as well as their feelings as they work toward the goal.

Criteria for Assessment:
a. Identifies an appropriate goal
b. Creates a realistic plan for meeting that goal
c. Identifies feelings experienced as they participated in the physical activity

Eighth Grade

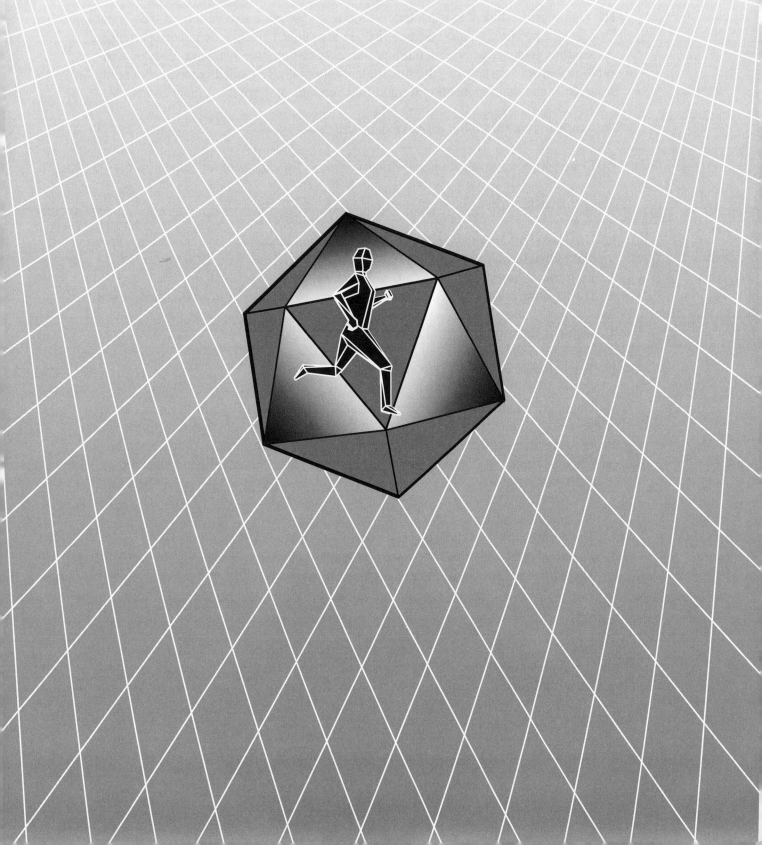

Eighth Grade

> **1. Demonstrates competency in many movement forms and proficiency in a few movement forms.**

The eighth grade student is expected to acquire competence in a variety of movement forms. As a result of an increased ability to vary skills, students are able to participate successfully in dance activities, outdoor pursuits, and modified versions of team and individual sports. In order to do this, students should have gained competence in the basic skills and their application to modified versions of these movement forms.

The emphasis for the eighth grade student will be to:

- Demonstrate competence in modified versions of a variety of movement forms.

Sample Benchmarks:

1. Uses basic offensive and defensive strategies in a modified version of a team sport and individual sport.
2. Performs a variety of simple folk and square dances.
3. Displays the basic skills and safety procedures to participate in an outdoor pursuit.

Assessment Examples:

1. Teacher observation - observational record

Students play a four-with-four person cooperative game of volleyball (four on each side of the net). The intent is for the players to keep the ball going back and forth across the net as many times as they can before it hits the floor. There must be at least two hits on each side before the ball can cross the net. When the ball hits the floor it must be restarted with a serve.

Criteria for Assessment:
a. The number of times the ball passes across the net
b. The number of combination passes and sets used by the teams
c. The number of successful serves

2. Group project

A group of eight students creates a performance using three dances of their choice that they have previously learned. They must practice until they are able to perform those dances without error.

Criteria for Assessment:
a. Performed correctly by all participants
b. Performed smoothly and with the appropriate rhythm

3. Portfolio

Students create a portfolio demonstrating competence in at least three different movement forms. Competence can be verified with videotape of performance or certification
of participation (e.g., softball All-stars; equestrian show, Red Cross certification).

Criteria for Assessment:
a. Demonstrates competence to participate safely in the activity
b. Exhibits the knowledge and basic skills necessary to be a regular participant in the
   activity

4. Formal skills test

AAHPERD test for basketball skills is used to assess speed spot shooting, passing, control dribble, and defensive movement (*Basketball for Boys and Girls: Skills Test
Manual*).

Criteria for Assessment:
a. Described in manual: Hopkins D, Shick L, and Plack J: *Basketball for Boys and
   Girls: Skills Test Manual*. Reston, 1984, AAHPERD.

2. Applies movement concepts and principles to the learning and development of motor skills.

The eighth grade student's increasing competence affords opportunities to develop more
advanced knowledge and understanding. This is exemplified through their growing
understanding and application of more advanced movement and game strategies, critical
elements of advanced movement skills, and the identification of characteristics representative of highly skilled performance. Concepts of practice in relation to performance
can be understood and applied and are indicative of the increasing complexity of discipline-specific knowledge that can be used (e.g., lengthening the lever increases linear
velocity).

The emphasis for the eighth grade student will be to:

• Understand and apply more advanced movement and game strategies.

• Identify the critical elements of more advanced movement skills.

• Identify the characteristics of highly skilled performance in a few movement forms.

• Understand and apply more advanced discipline specific knowledge.

Sample Benchmarks:

1. Explains and demonstrates some game strategies involved in playing tennis doubles.
2. Describes the critical elements of a racing start in freestyle swimming.
3. Having observed a team of elite volleyball players, describes the characteristics that enable success in serving, passing, and spiking.
4. Describes principles of training and conditioning for specific physical activities.

Assessment Examples:

1. Peer observation - observational record

One student is assigned to observe a modified game of tennis and to record points for the use of two different offensive strategies and one defensive strategy.

Criteria for Assessment:
a. Accurately observes and records the use of a strategy
b. Objectively observes both performers

2. Student project

Students will plan and teach a simple dance or game (selected from a movement form in which the student desires self-improvement) to a small group of fourth grade students. Students will be required to complete one or more of the following aspects of the project: (a) Develop a written plan that describes practice sessions appropriate for learning component skills and the activity as a whole. The plan should include practice of the movement patterns with each of the components (alone, partner, accompaniment, part, whole, stationery, moving, isolated skill, skill combinations). (b) Keep a journal reflecting the results of each practice session and adjustments that will be made for the next practice session. Summarize the experience by describing what was learned about how to learn a new skill.

Criteria for Assessment:
a. Correctly analyzes the activity to determine component skills and movement patterns
b. Selects appropriate practice procedures to learn and master skills and movement patterns of the activity
c. Uses information about performance to adjust practice procedures to improve skill performance
d. Appropriately records reflections of the performance to assess the learning process for the "teacher" and the "student"

3. Student report

Sports magazines contain a wealth of information concerning training tips and techniques related to various movement forms. Students are asked to go to the library and explore current issues of sports publications for articles related to a sport or activity of their choice. They should seek to find information about the critical elements of the skills inherent to the selected sport or activity, practice ideas for skill improvement, as

well as information about training and conditioning. Students will prepare a brief (at least one page per article) written summary of at least three articles on a movement form.

Criteria for Assessment:
a. Identifies motor fitness requirements of the selected physical activity
b. Identifies component skills and movement patterns of the selected activity or sport
c. Selects appropriate practice procedures to learn and master skills and movement patterns of the activity

4. Student project

Students select an activity in which they are currently participating or one in which they would like to participate. They are ask to develop a four-week training and conditioning program for this activity. Moreover, an analysis of the basic skills and movement patterns of the activity, an assessment of current skill and fitness status, a description of specific conditioning exercises and practice procedures, and goals for skill and fitness improvement should be included.

Criteria for Assessment:
a. Accurately assesses personal motor fitness status
b. Correctly identifies motor fitness requirements
c. Correctly identifies the component skills and movement patterns
d. Selects appropriate practice procedures to learn and master skills and movement patterns

3. Exhibits a physically active lifestyle.

The eighth grade student should be a participant in at least one physical activity outside of the school setting on a regular basis. It is the intent of this standard to increase awareness of the opportunities for participation and interest in participating in a broad range of different kinds of physical activity experiences. Students of this age should be able to independently set physical activity goals and participate in individualized programs of physical activity and exercise based on the results of fitness assessments, personal fitness goals, and interest. Greater and more specific understanding of long-term health benefits and understanding the relationship of health maintenance to the quality of lifelong health is expected.

The emphasis for the eighth grade student will be to:

• Establish personal physical activity goals.

• Participate regularly in health-enhancing physical activities to accomplish these goals (in and out of the physical education class.)

- Explore a variety of new physical activities for personal interest in and out of the physical education class.

- Describe the relationships between a healthy lifestyle and "feeling good."

Sample Benchmarks:

1. Participate in an individualized physical activity program designed with the help of the teacher.
2. List long-term physiological, psychological, and cultural benefits that may result from regular participation in physical activity.

Assessment Examples:

1. Student project

Undertake a planned personal exercise program designed with the help of the teacher. The program should reflect appropriate principles of practice and conditioning and be oriented so that it can be implemented at school, a local facility, or at home. The program should be designed to attain specific skill or health-related goals. Maintain a daily log indicating changes in fitness or performance levels. Continue participation until the desired goal is achieved or until a designated period of time has elapsed. The daily log should indicate feelings about the daily exercise. Upon completion, the student should complete a summary statement describing the results relative to the initial goal.

Criteria for Assessment:
a. Selects programs goals that are relevant and personally accurate
b. Applies principles of practice and conditioning appropriately
c. Maintains program throughout period of time
d. Achieves goals of program
e. Presents a well-organized and accurate log

2. Student project

Students are asked to identify two different activities available in the community with which they have no experience, but think they might enjoy. They must attend that activity first as an observer and later a participant, at least three times and write a report on that activity describing the activity, the equipment, the cost of participation (if any) and where the activity and instruction is available.

Criteria for Assessment:
a. Identifies two new activities
b. Attends the activity the assigned amount of time
c. Presents a well-organized and accurate report

3. Interview

Students are asked to select an adult who regularly engages in a personal activity program. Interview this person to determine what exercise they do, how long they have done it, why they do it, what motivates them to continue, and how they started. Students will then write a brief paper explaining their findings and what impact it has on them personally.

Criteria for Assessment:
a. Complete interview of selected individual
b. Prepares an accurate paper based on interview
c. Presents appropriate synthesis of information and conclusions

4. Group project

Using resources in the school library, the public health department or a local hospital or university, plan a physical activity fair. All students in the class can be involved or they can work in smaller groups on related projects. Students will individually select appropriate topics to allow them to select speakers, create displays or plan for other activities that would benefit the fair.

Criteria for Assessment:
a. Demonstrates an understanding of the value of an active lifestyle
b. Completes their assigned project
c. Project reflects group cohesiveness, enthusiasm, and creativity

4. Achieves and maintains a health-enhancing level of physical fitness.

Students at this level should participate in physical activities that address each component of health-related fitness, including muscular strength and endurance, flexibility, body composition, as well as cardiorespiratory endurance. They can assess their personal fitness status for each component. Students are introduced to the various principles of training (e.g., threshold, overload, specificity) and how they can be utilized in improving physical fitness. At this level, students should be able to interpret the results of physical fitness assessments and use this information to assist in the development of individualized physical fitness goals with little assistance from the teacher.

The emphasis for the eighth grade student will be to:

• Participate in a variety of health-related fitness activities in both school and non-school settings.

• Assess physiological indicators of exercise during and after physical activity.

• Understand and apply basic principles of training to improving physical fitness.

- Begin to develop personal fitness goals independently.

- Meet the health-related fitness standards as defined by Fitnessgram.

Sample Benchmarks:

1. Maintains a record of moderate to vigorous physical activity.
2. Correctly demonstrates various weight training techniques.
3. Plans a circuit weight training program designed to meet physical fitness goals.
4. Participates in fitness-enhancing physical activities outside of school (e.g., gymnastic clubs, community sponsored youth sports).
5. Engages in physical activity at the target heart rate for a minimum of 20 minutes.

Assessment Examples:

1. Student log

Students maintain a log or diary of their physical activity for 7 consecutive days. In order to allow for seasonal variation in activity, this log should be maintained periodically throughout the year.

Criteria for Assessment:
a. Completes log for 7 consecutive days on at least three occasions during the school year
b. Records accurate information regarding the type of activity, duration, frequency, and intensity of participation
c. Includes both in-school and out-of-school activities in the log

2. Formal test

The student participates in the Fitnessgram Physical Fitness Test and meets the criteria established for their age and gender.

3. Student project

Using the results of the fall fitness test as baseline information, students develop a 6-week plan for improving their fitness level on their weakest component.

Criteria for Assessment:
a. Correctly interprets personal information from fitness test results in order to identify the component of fitness needing most improvement
b. Selects appropriate activities for improving their status on the fitness component needing remediation
c. Demonstrates an understanding of basic exercise training principles such as frequency, intensity, duration and mode of exercise

4. Student report

Following instructions for taking one's own pulse, students monitor their heart rate before, during, and immediately following a variety of physical activities performed during class. Students prepare a written report describing the physiological response to exercise, providing their own heart rate information as a basis for illustrating the body's response to a minimum of three different activities. (This activity could be modified to use a heart rate monitor instead of palpation for determining heart rate.)

Criteria for Assessment:
a. Accurately takes their own pulse at rest and during exercise
b. Demonstrates an understanding of selected physiological responses to exercise (e.g., increased heart rate, heavy breathing, sweating) in the written report
c. Correctly differentiates the body's response to physical activities of various exercise intensities

5. Student project

Students are asked to estimate their own maximal heart rate (220 minus age), determine their resting heart rate through carotid or radial artery palpation, and then determine their heart rate reserve. Based on this information, students determine the optimum cardiovascular training zone by computing the training intensities at 70 percent and 85 percent of their heart rate reserve.

Criteria for Assessment:
a. Accurately determines maximal heart rate, resting heart rate and heart rate reserve
b. Determines appropriate cardiovascular training zone

5. Demonstrates responsible personal and social behavior in physical activity settings

Students are beginning to seek greater independence from adults. They make appropriate decisions to resolve conflicts arising from the powerful influence of peers and to follow pertinent practices, rules, and procedures necessary for successful performance. They practice appropriate problem-solving techniques to resolve conflicts when necessary in competitive activities. Students reflect on the benefits of the role of rules, procedures, safe practices, ethical behavior, and positive social interaction in physical activity settings.

The emphasis for the eighth grade student will be to:

• Recognize the influence of peer pressure.

• Solve problems by analyzing causes and potential solutions.

- Analyze potential consequences when confronted with a behavior choice.

- Work cooperatively with a group to achieve group goals in competitive as well as cooperative settings.

Sample Benchmarks:

1. Identifies positive and negative peer influence.
2. Plays within the rules of a game or activity.
3. Considers the consequences when confronted with a behavior choice.
4. Resolves interpersonal conflicts with a sensitivity to rights and feelings of others.
5. Handles conflicts that arise with others without confrontation.
6. Finds positive ways to exert independence.
7. Tempers the desire to "belong" to a peer group with a growing awareness of independent thought.
8. Makes choices based on the safety of self and others.
9. Accepts a controversial decision of an official.

Assessment Examples:

1. Teacher observation - observational record

The teacher observes students' performances during class and records the instances of unsafe behavior or undesirable behavior in an activity (e.g., crashing into a gymnastics apparatus, arguing with a peer.)

Criteria for Assessment:
a. Participates in a manner that is safe for himself or herself
b. Participates in a manner that is safe for others
c. Exhibits appropriate self-control and good sportsmanship during activity

2. Event task - observational record

During a team game a designated official will score both the game points and the "behavior points." Students get one behavior point for every overt example of supportive, ethical behavior and lose one behavior point for every example to the contrary. Individual and team points may be kept.

Criteria for Assessment:
a. Demonstrates supportive behavior to a teammate or opponent (e.g., verbal feedback, nonverbal feedback, helping a student up who has fallen, perform skills at the highest level possible.)

3. Student journal

After each class period the student records in a journal examples of their behavior in

which they displayed good sportsmanship and examples in which they did not display good sportsmanship.

Criteria for Assessment:
a. Accurately records those behaviors that are positive or negative examples of sportsmanship.
b. Increases the number of positive examples and decreases the number of negative examples of sportsmanship over time.

4. Student project

Students are asked to create a list of actions, both positive and negative in nature, that they have observed during involvement in physical activity over the past week for each of the behaviors listed below. For those actions considered to be negative, suggest an alternative action that would be considered to be more appropriate.

Behavior	Action	Alternative Action
Conflict with peer		
Language		
Preparation		
Promptness		
Safety		
Support for Others		

Criteria for Assessment:
a. Provides satisfactory examples of indicated behaviors
b. Correctly ascertains if action is positive or negative
c. Selects appropriate alternative actions

6. Demonstrates understanding and respect for differences among people in physical activity settings

Beginning in the eighth grade, the concept of physical activity as a microcosm of modern culture and society is introduced. Students should be able to recognize the role of physical activity in understanding diversity in modern culture. Students continue to include and support each other and respect the limitations and strengths of group members.

The emphasis for the eighth grade student will be to:

• Recognize the role of sport, games, and dance in modern culture.

• Identify behaviors that are supportive and inclusive in physical activity settings.

• Willingly join others of diverse culture, ethnicity, and race during physical activity.

Sample Benchmarks:

1. Demonstrates an understanding of the ways sport and dance influence American culture.
2. Displays sensitivity to the feelings of others during interpersonal interactions.
3. Respects the physical and performance limitations of self and others.

Assessment Examples:

1. Student project

The images of sport celebrities portrayed through the media often affect the behavior of those who watch or read about these celebrities. Students are asked to choose two famous athletes—one who is generally admired for his or her positive behavior and one who is known generally for his or her negative behavior. Students should compare and contrast the images portrayed by these athletes and comment on the effect the images have on their own behavior or the behavior of others their age.

Criteria for Assessment:
a. Identifies both positive and negative sport celebrity behaviors
b. Identifies cultural changes brought about by these sport "heroes"
c. Provides evidence that supports a comparative description of the two athletes
d. Recognizes the effect that these athletes may have on the behavior of others

2. Student project

Students are asked to identify the predominant minority populations in their school, local community, or state. Based on this information, students are requested to learn a game or dance native to one of those populations. (See if classmates can guess which country it is from based on the activity, music, costume, etc.)

Criteria for Assessment:
a. Identifies characteristics that make the activity unique and distinguishable
b. Notes similarities with games or dances from other areas
c. Works with both high and low skilled individuals to learn new games and dances

3. Student journal

Exclusionary behavior during physical activity can be very subtle. Students are asked to observe physical activity during physical education class or on the playground and record instances of perceived exclusionary behavior. For example, the methods used to choose teams are often exclusionary, differences in ability level can lead to exclusionary behavior such as failing to pass to less skilled players in a basketball game, or exclusion related to gender or cultural/ethnic differences. In addition, students are asked to suggest strategies for maximizing inclusion in physical activity settings.

Criteria for Assessment:
a. Identifies instances of exclusionary behavior
b. Formulates strategies for maximizing inclusionary behavior (e.g., by changing the rules of the activity)
c. Provides evidences of sensitivity to those of different gender, culture, race, and physical ability

7. Understands that physical activity provides the opportunity for enjoyment, challenge, self-expression, and social interaction.

A primary reason eighth graders seek physical activity is for group membership and positive social interaction. Physical activities provide a positive outlet for competition with peers and a means of gaining the respect and recognition of others. Skill expertise is increasingly valued. Physical activity can increase self-confidence and self-esteem as students discover renewed enjoyment of participation. Feelings of independence are beginning to be important as well. Physical activities can provide confidence as students start to take steps toward independence. Challenge is found in both high levels of competition as well as in new or different activities. As students experience a greater awareness of feelings, the avenues of self-expression provided by dance, gymnastics, and various sport activities become increasingly more important.

The emphasis for the eighth grade student will be to:

• Enjoy participation in physical activity.

• Recognize the social benefits of participation in physical activity.

• Try new and challenging activities.

• Recognize physical activity as a vehicle for self-expression

Sample Benchmarks:

1. Feels satisfaction when engaging in physical activity.
2. Enjoys the aesthetic and creative aspects of performance.
3. Enjoys learning new activities.
4. Becomes more skilled (e.g., learning strategy, additional skills) in a favorite activity.

Assessment Examples:

1. Student report

After participating in both a team and individual or dual sport activity, students write an essay discussing the differences of opportunities for social interaction in each. Possible topics to explore might include, but are not be limited to: Which did the student prefer? Why? What activities does the student participate in with friends? How are social factors important in the selection of an activity?

Criteria for Assessment:
a. Recognizes the social benefits of participation in physical activity

b. Identifies the differences in social aspects of team and individual sports
c. Identifies reasons for enjoying participation

2. Student project

Students are asked to a) identify those incidents in sport/activity participation (in or out of physical education class) that made them feel really good and those that made then feel really bad, and b) describe what they have learned about how to create positive experiences for themselves and others in sport/physical activity.

Criteria for Assessment:
a. Identifies experiences appropriately according to the positive and negative feelings they have evoked
b. Demonstrates insight into how to create positive experiences for self and others

3. Journal

Following a discussion with students regarding situations that are stressful, students are requested to participate in some form of physical activity after the next stressful situation they encounter. Have them describe in their journal the feelings during and after this stressful experience and whether or not exercise helped to relieve the tension. They should also record the type of activity in which they participated. Does the activity have to be strenuous in order to be stress-relieving?

Criteria for Assessment:
a. Recognizes the value of exercise in relieving stress
b. Recognizes when or if exercise helped in relieving the stress
c. Identifies some activities as more stress-reducing than others

4. Student project - essay

Students are asked to write a newspaper review (like a critique) of a local dance performance they observed.

Criteria for Assessment:
a. Demonstrates an awareness of the qualities of good aesthetic performance
b. Identifies how the dancers communicated with the audience during the performance
c. Notes the self-expression from the dancers as they danced

Tenth Grade

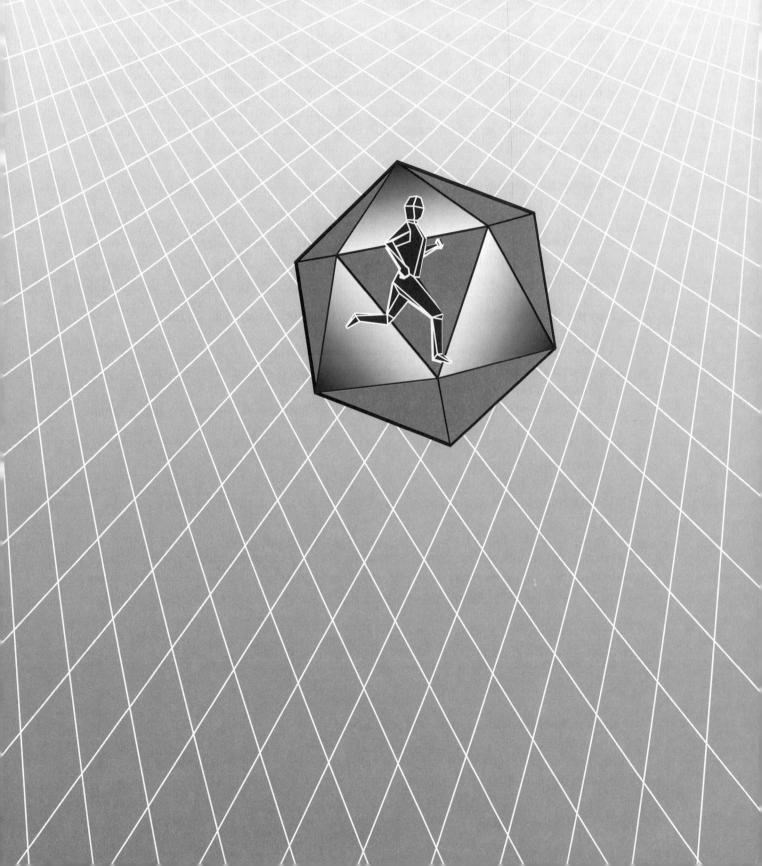

Tenth Grade

1. Demonstrates competency in many movement forms and proficiency in a few movement forms.

Tenth grade students should increase the number of activities for which they have acquired a level of competence. Furthermore, these activities should represent a variety of movement forms. Whereas prior to this time, competence was often achieved within modified versions of various movement forms, the tenth grade student should be capable of achieving competency in more complex versions of movement forms. Competency involves the ability to use the basic skills, strategies and rules of an activity to a degree of success that makes the activity enjoyable.

The emphasis for the tenth grade student will be to:

- Demonstrate competence (basic skills, strategies and rules) in an increasing number of more complex versions of at least three of the following different types of movement forms: aquatics, team sports, individual and dual sports, outdoor pursuits, self-defense, dance, gymnastics.

Sample Benchmarks:

1. Demonstrates a variety of proficient swimming strokes.
2. Uses a variety of clubs competently to play a round of golf.
3. Is competent with a variety of social dance forms.
4. Keeps a ball going with an opponent several times over the net in a game of tennis.
5. Plays a game of volleyball using all the basic skills and strategies of the sport.

Assessment Examples:

1. Portfolio

Students will develop a portfolio documenting their ability to be competent in three different types of movement forms. Support can be a videotape of performance, certificate from a recognized sport agency (e.g., Red Cross certification) or acceptable grade on a written and skill evaluation.

Criteria for Assessment:
a. Three different types of movement forms are supported
b. Level of ability in a movement form shows competence
c. Presents adequate documentation in portfolio

2. Teacher observation - observational record

Students are observed performing an activity or executing skills inherent to the activity and are rated on their level of competence using a teacher-designed rating scale or scoring rubric.

Criteria for Assessment:

a. Exhibits a level of competency with all of the basic skills of the activity and the ability to use these skills with some consistency in the appropriate setting
b. Demonstrates understanding of the rules and strategies of a sport or activity and can apply them appropriately
c. Displays appropriate etiquette, ways of interacting, care of equipment, and safety in the setting of an activity

3. Formal Skills Test

Teacher administers American Red Cross level 4 swimming skills test.

2. Applies movement concepts and principles to the learning and development of motor skills.

Students at this grade level are beginning to specialize in a few movement forms leading toward proficiency. Achieving this level of ability requires more specialized knowledge and the identification and application of critical elements essential to competent/proficient performance. They are increasingly capable of identifying and applying characteristics of highly skilled performance. This student should be able to understand and independently apply increasingly complex discipline-specific information to their own performance.

The emphasis for the tenth grade student will be to:

• Use more specialized knowledge to develop movement competence or proficiency .

• Identify and apply critical elements to enable the development of movement competence/proficiency.

• Identify and apply characteristics of highly skilled performance to enable the development of movement competence/proficiency.

• Understand and independently apply discipline specific information to their own performance.

Sample Benchmarks:

1. Performs a variety of dance forms (e.g., folk, country, social, and creative) with fluency and in time to accompaniment.
2. Applies biomechanical concepts and principles to analyze and improve performance of self and others.
3. Devises and performs a gymnastics routine after explaining the significance of some

biomechanical principles to the skills involved.
4. Describes and demonstrates the significance of some basic physiological principles to the development of a personal fitness program.

Assessment Examples:

1. Group project

In groups of three or four, students select a physical activity and analyze it for its component skills and movement patterns. Specifically, students should complete the following in relation to that analysis: (a) Create routines, drills, or small games that focus on individual skills, themes, or strategies, and that provide practice within the context of the movement form. (Example: bump the serve accurately to a front line player for a successful set and spike at the net. The team scores a point each time the whole sequence is completed successfully.) (b) Plan practice sessions appropriate for developing each of the skills, including the skill status, system for tracking progress, achievement goals of members of the group, and the length and frequency of practice sessions. (c) Implement the plan. (d) Report the results, including progress made by each member of the group.

Criteria for Assessment:
a. Component skills are correctly identified for the selected activity
b. Routines, skills, and games are developed appropriately for the movement activity
c. Plan developed for practice uses information from a variety of sources appropriately
d. Records of practice and performance are kept accurately and used appropriately to assess progress.

2. Student project

Students will videotape themselves performing a sport skill, dance, or other physical activity of their choice, analyze the performance, and prepare a written report that includes one or more of the following: (a) a listing of all the skills and strategies used; (b) analysis of personal performance of the skills shown on the tape; (c) a listing of the positive and negative performance attributes observed for each skill; (d) a listing of the critical elements for successful performance within the context of the activity; (e) suggested practice procedures that might be used to improve performance in the skills and strategies to improve overall performance in the activity; (f) suggest a conditioning program to enhance performance of the skills involved.

Criteria for Assessment:
a. Skills and strategies used in the activity are correctly identified
b. Positive and negative aspects of personal performance are correctly identified.
c. Identifies correctly the critical elements for successful performance within the context of the activity
d. Describes appropriate practice procedures to improve skill and strategy of the activity
e. Develops an appropriate conditioning program for the selected activity

3.   Teacher observation - observational record

The more skilled students in a class are given the responsibility to improve the performance of the less skilled students on a particular skill. They are asked to observe, assess, and coach the practice of this skill for three consecutive class periods and then to assess the improvement in performance.

Criteria for Assessment:
a. Accurately identifies the strengths and weaknesses of performance.
b. Designs appropriate practice sessions to improve performance.
c. Maintains peer motivation to improve through positive interaction.

3. Exhibits a physically active lifestyle.

Students in the tenth grade should have the skills and knowledge to assess and develop their own personal physical activity program and the desire to carry it through. Emphasis is placed on providing students the opportunity to analyze the benefits of their own activity program in relationship to personal interests, capabilities, and needs. Students at this level should be able to develop sound strategies for incorporating physical activity into a comprehensive lifetime activity plan. Students should be able to locate and arrange opportunities for physical activities within the community and surrounding areas and should be participants outside the physical education setting on a regular basis.

The emphasis for the tenth grade student will be to:

•   Participate regularly in health-enhancing and personally rewarding physical activity outside the physical education class setting.

•   Seek and select physical activities from a variety of movement forms based on personal interest, meaning and fulfillment.

•   Develop and conduct independently a personal physical activity program meeting their needs.

Sample Benchmarks:

1. Participates in health-enhancing activities that can be pursued in the community.
2. Analyzes and evaluates personal fitness profile.
3. Identifies personal behavior that supports and does not support a healthy lifestyle.
4. Analyzes and compares health and fitness benefits derived from various physical activities.

Assessment Examples:

1. Student journal

For one month the student keeps a daily journal of participation in physical activity. The student records information like the contributions of activity to maintaining physical fitness (e.g., aerobic endurance, flexibility, strength), feelings about physical and psychological well-being before, during, and after the activity. At the end of one month, the student summarizes findings by answering questions like the following:

Are you exercising enough to maintain a healthy lifestyle?
Does your current level of selection of activities generally leave you with a sense of satisfaction, fulfillment, and enjoyment?

Based on answers to each of these questions, make suggestions for maintaining or changing current exercise patterns to achieve desired benefits.

Criteria for Assessment:
a. Participates regularly in health-enhancing physical activities
b. Analyzes benefits of selected physical activities
c. Identifies and reflects on feelings of personal benefit that result from participation in specific physical activities

2. Student journal

Students select and participate in a community based, health-enhancing physical activity. They are asked to keep a journal for a prescribed period of time showing participation time, type of activity selected, costs, facilities employed, equipment required, personnel involved, and related factors that impact the student's ability to participate.

Criteria for Assessment:
a. Participates at least three times per week in appropriate health-enhancing activities
b. Solves problems that limit or prohibit participation

3. Class project

Students are asked to survey the community to determine possible opportunities for participation in health-enhancing physical activities. This information could be gathered from the logs that class members prepared in the previous assessment example.

Criteria for Assessment:
a. Selects health-enhancing activities
b. Identifies factors that enable or restrict participation
c. Suggests plan of action to increase accessibility
d. Applies communication and citizenship skills and knowledge to initiate action to increase community accessibility to activity programs

4. Student report

The student chooses four accessible, community-based, physical activities of personal interest. For each activity the student describes the potential social, psychological, and physical benefits.

Criteria for Assessment:
a. Analyzes physical activities for their health-enhancing potential.
b. Seeks and selects physical activities based on personal interest, meaning, and fulfillment.
c. Identifies opportunities to share and learn from others through physical activity.

5. Portfolio

Students create individual charts showing a list of physical activities in which they have participated within the past six months. These activities could have been community or school-based and could have been individual, group, or family activities. For each activity the students should indicate: (1) their personal feeling toward the activity, (2) their perceived level of competence, (3) the health, fitness, and skill requirements of the activity, and (4) their current personal health, fitness, and skill status relative to the activity. Each student should submit a portfolio with the chart. The portfolio should include various types of information documenting the information on the chart (e.g., ribbons awarded from competitions, photographs of the student participating, videotape showing level of ability.) The portfolio should provide evidence of the extent of participation, the student participating in various types of activities, awareness of the benefits of the activity, and skill development.

Criteria for Assessment:
a. Seeks and selects physical activities based on personal interest, meaning, and fulfillment.
b. Analyzes physical activities on the basis of personal interest, capability, and potential for success.
c. Identifies and reflects on feelings of personal benefit that result from regular participation in physical activity.

4. Achieves and maintains a health-enhancing level of physical fitness.

Tenth grade students should begin to choose and participate on a regular basis in physical activities that enable them to achieve and maintain health-related fitness. Students work to improve fitness levels by applying principles of training to participation in exercise and physical activities chosen with a specific training intent. Students should be able to interpret information from fitness tests and begin to design, with teacher guidance, personal programs to achieve and maintain health-related fitness goals.

The emphasis for the tenth grade student will be to:

- Participate in a variety of health-enhancing physical activities in both school and nonschool settings.

- Use principles of training for the purpose of modifying levels of fitness.

- Assess personal health-related fitness status.

- Begin to design personal health-related fitness programs based on an accurately assessed fitness profile.

- Meet the health-related fitness standards as defined by Fitnessgram.

Sample Benchmarks:

1. Assesses personal fitness status in terms of cardiovascular endurance, muscular strength and endurance, flexibility, and body composition.
2. Designs and implements a personal fitness program.
3. Participates in a variety of physical activities appropriate for enhancing physical fitness.
4. Evaluates personal fitness profile.
5. Meets personal fitness goals after a period of training.

Assessment Examples:

1. Formal test

The student participates in the Fitnessgram Physical Fitness Test and meets the criteria established for their age and gender.

2. Student project

The student assesses their own fitness level on the basis of the results of the physical fitness testing conducted during the Fall term. This assessment should enable the student to identify those aspects of fitness that warrant improvement as well as those that simply need to be maintained. Based on this assessment, the student establishes personal fitness goals and designs a fitness training program that would enable him or her to achieve the specified goals over a period of 3 months. At the end of 3 months the student assesses the extent to which the goals have been met.

Criteria for Assessment:
a. Accurately assesses their current level of fitness.
b. Establishes realistic yet challenging goals.
c. Designs a program that has the potential to meet the identified goals.
d. Accurately assesses the degree to which the goals have been attained.

3. Teacher observation - observational record

The teacher observes students participating on a circuit weight-training program to assure the proper application of selected weight-training principles (e.g., specificity of training, overload principle, mode of training, resistance, sets). Incidents of improper use of training principles are recorded and discussed with the student.

Criteria for Assessment:
a. Demonstrates appropriate application of selected weight-training principles
b. Improves performance on tests of muscular strength and endurance following training period. (Tests such as a 1 RM lift on various stations, 60-second curl-up, modified pull-up, and push-ups may be used to assess muscular strength and endurance.)

4. Student project

The student develops a "Fitness Concepts Notebook" that contains a definition of physical fitness, a description of the various components of physical fitness and exercises and activities (appropriate for this age) designed to maintain or improve these components, and a discussion of the training principles that affect the development of each of the health-related aspects of physical fitness. Drawings or illustrations taken from magazines or newspapers may be used to depict the various exercises and activities recommended.

Criteria for Assessment:
a. Provides a correct definition of physical fitness and cites appropriate fitness components.
b. Presents age-appropriate exercises that will enhance the various components of physical fitness.
c. Discusses a minimum of two training principles appropriate for enhancing flexibility, muscular strength and endurance, and cardiorespiratory endurance.

5. Demonstrates responsible personal and social behavior in physical activity settings

Students demonstrate responsible personal and social behavior by following safe practices, rules, procedures, and etiquette in all physical activity settings with an understanding of their responsibility as a positive influence on the behavior of others. They should be able to respond to potentially explosive interactions with others in a controlled fashion. Students should be able to evaluate competitive activities based on a variety of goals.

The emphasis for the tenth grade student will be to:

• Apply safe practices, rules, procedures, and etiquette in all physical activity settings.

• Act independently of peer pressure.

- Resolve conflicts in appropriate ways.

- Keep the importance of winning and losing in perspective relative to other established goals of participation.

Sample Benchmarks:

1. Slides into a base in a manner that avoids injury to the defensive player.
2. Chooses an activity because they enjoy it and not because all their friends are in it.
3. Volunteers to replay a contested shot in tennis.
4. Walks away from verbal confrontation.
5. Acknowledges good play from an opponent during competition.
6. Listens to all sides before taking action in conflict situations.

Assessment Examples:

1. Self-assessment

After playing a self-officiated game, students discuss and report on ethical, fair play and supportive behavior they exhibited during the game.

Criteria for Assessment:
a. Recognizes elements of fair play, honesty, and ethical behavior in their own performance
b. Accepts the roles and decisions of the officials
c. Shows a sensitivity to the feelings of other players
d. Demonstrates an acceptance of the importance of rules and players following them

2. Written test

Students take a written test that focuses on safety rules and procedures for in-class activities.

Criteria for Assessment:
a. Identifies several rules and procedures that are designed for safe participation
b. Explains why and how a rule makes participation safe

3. Student project

At the beginning of a unit of instruction, students are requested to analyze their potential for success and set goals for personal achievement. At the end of the unit, students prepare an evaluation of their progress towards their personal goals and cite influences on their achievement to date.

Criteria for Assessment:

a. Sets realistic goals
b. Correctly assesses their progress towards the goals
c. Identifies appropriate factors influencing their achievement
d. Accepts personal responsibility for level of achievement

4. Student report

Students are asked to prepare a report that describes a confrontation involving sport participants that they have observed or read about. The report should describe the resolution of the confrontation and discuss possible factors that led to the confrontation as well as suggest ways in which the confrontation could have been avoided.

Criteria for Assessment:
a. Identifies a situation that involves a confrontation between participants
b. Correctly analyzes the causes of the problem
c. Suggests meaningful potential solutions

6. Demonstrates understanding and respect for differences among people in physical activity settings

By the tenth grade, students should be able to understand and analyze the role of sport and physical activity in a diverse world. Insight is gained through such activities as exploration of the history and purposes of various international competitions (e.g., Special Olympics, Pan American Games, World Cup Soccer), the role of professional sport in society, effects of age and gender on participation patterns, and the usefulness of dance as an expression of multiculturalism. Students begin to develop a personal philosophy concerning inclusive participation in physical activity.

The emphasis for the tenth grade student will be to:

* Recognize the value of sport and physical activity in understanding multiculturalism.

* Invite others with differences (e.g., ethnicity, gender, disabilities) to join in personally enjoyable physical activity.

Sample Benchmarks:

1. Discusses the historical roles of games, sports, and dance in the cultural life of a population.
2. Enjoys the satisfaction of meeting and cooperating with others of diverse backgrounds during physical activity.

Assessment Examples:

1. Videotape - observational record

The teacher sets up a videotape in a corner of the space or playing field from which he or she can view the entire class in an activity where there is a great deal of interaction between students. In reviewing the tape, the teacher looks for evidence of inclusive and discriminatory behavior.

Criteria for Assessment:
a. Recognizes students who do not feel included and makes a deliberate effort to include them in some way.
b. Does not participate in exclusionary behavior

2. Student report

The role of women in sport in the United States has gone through a significant transition since 1960. Students are asked to describe the history of women in sport in the United States with particular emphasis on the transitions occurring from 1960 to the present. The report should also include examples of female athletes who have contributed to the transitions as well as a discussion of how these transitions reflect the evolution of women's issues in American society at large.

Criteria for Assessment:
a. Recognizes the effect of changing cultural values that have led to increased female sport participation
b. Cites legislative reasons for increase in female participation and opportunity
c. Gives several examples of female sport pioneers

3. Group project

Working in small groups, students are asked to research popular games that children use as play in various diverse cultures and then teach these games to young children at an activity center or elementary school. Alternatively, have a festival or "multicultural Olympics" at school and teach others to play these games. Upon completion of this activity students would discuss the following during oral reporting to the class: What do these games have in common? What are the differences? What do these games tell us about the social values and cultures of the originating countries? What are the challenges in teaching these games to a diverse population?

Criteria for Assessment:
a. Identifies several popular games from various cultures
b. Uses games to interact with others
c. Adapts games for the diverse population found in most schools
d. Understands how play and games are part of a culture and is able to explain this to others

7. Understands that physical activity provides the opportunity for enjoyment, challenge, self-expression, and social interaction.

Tenth graders are beginning to feel more comfortable with their new interests and physiques, thus once again enjoying movement for the sheer pleasure of moving. In addition, they enjoy the challenge of working hard to better their skills and feel satisfaction when they are successful in improving. Members of competitive teams and those involved in groups experience the positive feelings associated through working with others to achieve a distant goal (e.g., winning a team championship.) Students also experience satisfaction and enjoyment while pursuing personal goals.

The emphasis for the tenth grade student will be to:

- Enjoy participating in a variety of physical activities in competitive and recreational settings

- Pursue new activities both alone or with others.

- Enjoy working with others in a sport activity to achieve a common goal.

- Recognize that physical activity can provide a positive social environment for activities with others.

Sample Benchmarks:

1. Identifies participation factors that contribute to enjoyment and self-expressions
2. Contributes meaningfully to the achievement of a team

Assessment Examples:

1. Written report

Students are requested to write a dialogue convincing a friend to try out for or participate in a sport or activity. The dialogue should highlight the reasons that participation can be enjoyable, from both a physical and social standpoint. In addition, the dialogue should try to anticipate the negative factors that would lead one to not want to participate or join a team and address these in a positive fashion.

Criteria for Assessment:
a. Identifies enjoyment and challenge as some of the reasons to participate in the activity
b. Indicates that the positive aspects far outweigh the negative ones
c. Identifies several benefits of participation in physical activity

2. Journal

During an adventure education experience (e.g., ropes course, climbing a wall, nature hikes, camping, canoeing), students shall record in a journal the feelings and thoughts they experienced throughout.

Criteria for Assessment:
a. Demonstrates awareness of feelings and ability to translate these into journal
b. Provides evidence of success, challenge, and enjoyment that were present in the experience
c. Recognizes the unique benefits of this type of physical activity experience
d. Recognizes the positive effects friends and companions bring to this experience

3. Student project

The student chooses to do a dance as a way to interpret a poem or reading.

Criteria for Assessment:
a. Recognizes dance as a means of communicating and expressing feelings
b. Translates the written work into movement forms
c. Shows enjoyment as the project is presented

Twelfth Grade

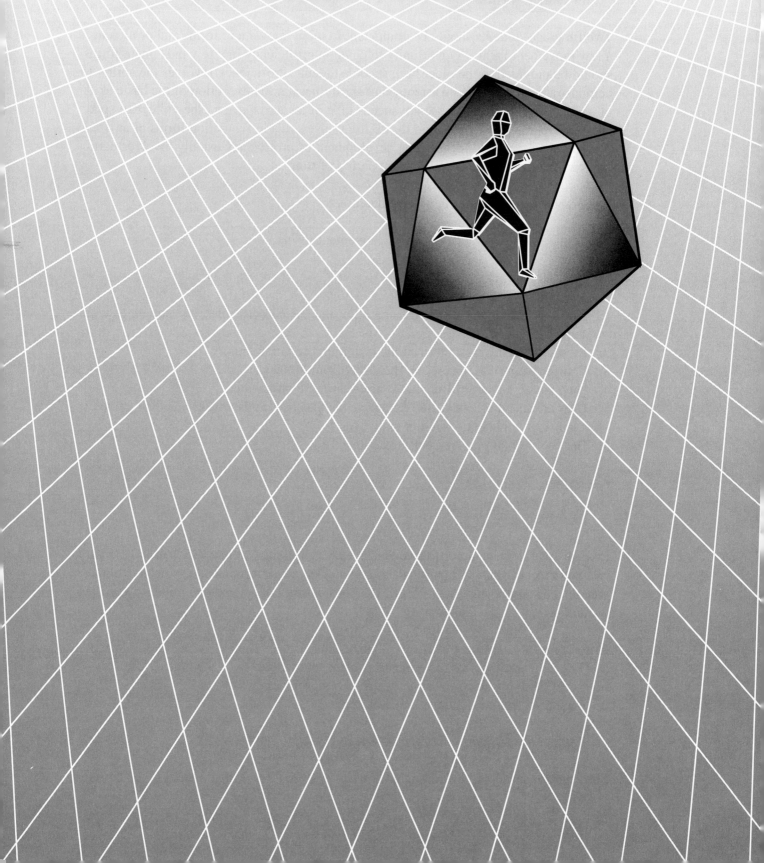

Twelfth Grade

1. Demonstrates competency in many movement forms and proficiency in a few movement forms.

Twelfth grade students should be competent in many movement forms and proficient in a few movement forms. Opportunity to develop proficiency in a few movement forms should be provided to the older high school student. Proficiency involves the ability to demonstrate a degree of consistency and skillfulness in the execution of the basic skills of an activity, the ability to use advanced skills of an activity (e.g., the volleyball spike, cut dropshot in badminton), and the ability to use skills in regulation forms of an activity rather than modified forms. The development of proficiency usually involves participation in that activity for an extended period of time.

The emphasis for the twelfth grade student is to:

- Demonstrate proficiency in a few movement forms.

Sample Benchmarks:

1. Participates in a tennis match using all of the basic skills, rules, and strategies with some consistency.
2. Passes the Red Cross intermediate swimming requirements.
3. Can get 9 out of 10 arrows on the target from 40 feet.
4. Navigates a kayak skillfully and safely through whitewater.
5. Uses advanced offensive and defensive shots successfully in a racquetball game against an opponent of similar skill.
6. Has the skills for a black belt in karate.

Assessment Examples:

1. Portfolio

Students will develop a portfolio documenting their ability to be proficient in at least two movement forms. Support can be a videotape of performance, certificate from a recognized sport agency (e.g., Red Cross certification) or acceptable grade on a written evaluation and skill evaluation.

Criteria for Assessment:
a. Two different types of movement forms are supported
b. Level of ability in a movement form shows proficiency
c. Presents adequate documentation in portfolio

2. Teacher observation - observational record

Students are observed performing an activity or executing skills inherent to the activity and are rated on their level of competence using a teacher-designed rating scale or scoring rubric.

Criteria for Assessment:
a. Exhibits a level of proficiency with all of the basic skills of the activity and the ability to use these skills with some consistency in the appropriate setting
b. Demonstrates understanding of the rules and strategies of a sport or activity and can apply them appropriately
c. Displays appropriate etiquette, ways of interacting/care of equipment, and safety in the setting of an activity

2. Applies movement concepts and principles to the learning and development of motor skills.

The twelfth grade student should be able to demonstrate the knowledge and understanding necessary to develop scientifically based personal training programs and implement effective practice procedures for proficient performance in a few movement forms. In addition, they should be able to independently understand and apply advanced discipline-specific information. Advanced activity related to discipline-specific knowledge is integrated so that the student develops the ability to learn, self-assess, and improve movement skills independently.

The emphasis for the twelfth grade student will be to:

*   Know and understand pertinent scientifically based information regarding movement performance.

*   Independently apply advanced movement-specific information.

*   Integrate discipline-specific knowledge to enable the independent learning of movement skills.

Sample Benchmarks:

1. Explains the overload principle and designs a personal fitness program where this principle is in operation.
2. Demonstrates several skills in gymnastics before explaining some biomechanical principles that govern the movement.
3. Designs a long-term plan for self-improvement in a movement activity and explains the relationship of physical, emotional, and cognitive factors that influence the rate of improvement.
4. Uses internal and external information to modify movement during performance.

Assessment Examples:

1. Written test

Students are administered an essay examination testing their understanding of the physiological principles (e.g., overload principle, law of specificity) governing fitness maintenance and improvement. At least one test item is specifically designed to test the student's ability to practically apply this knowledge to a training program for a specific activity.

Criteria for Assessment:
a. Understands pertinent physiological principles governing fitness
b. Applies knowledge of physiological principles to a specific activity/sport.

2. Student project

Using a school or home video camera, the student makes a ten to fifteen minute video production illustrating elite performance of a variety of movement activities. The student narrates the tape describing the pertinent principles from motor learning and development, exercise physiology, biomechanics, or sport psychology that govern the movements being shown on the tape.

Criteria for Assessment:
a. Recognizes elite level performance
b. Identifies pertinent scientific principles governing specific movement activities

3. Student report - oral presentation

Students select a movement activity that they plan to pursue following graduation and complete a library search on the psychological considerations that govern performance in this activity. These factors and their effects are then explained to the class in a 10-minute oral presentation.

Criteria for Assessment:
a. Correctly identifies the psychological factors that govern movement performance of the selected activity
b. Applies pertinent psychological factors to the specific movement activity

4. Student report - written report or oral presentation

Students will select and interview an adult who is an elite-level performer in a particular movement activity. The purpose of the interview is to determine what elite performers know about the scientific factors and principles that affect their performance. Upon completion of the interview, the student will prepare a five-page written paper or present a 10-minute oral report to the class describing the factors that the athlete believes affects the quality of their performance. Furthermore, discuss any additional factors that you think the athlete may have omitted.

Criteria for Assessment:

a. Selects an elite-level athlete and obtains appropriate information during the interview

b. Correctly assesses the accuracy of the information identified by the athlete and supplements information as warranted

c. Communicates the information gathered during the interview in an effective manner

3. Exhibits a physically active lifestyle.

By the twelfth grade the student should fully recognize and understand the significance of physical activity in the maintenance of a healthy lifestyle and should have developed the skills, interest and desire to maintain an active lifestyle. They should also assume a mature role in managing their participation in physical activity. They should feel fully empowered to make choices between those activities that are and are not personally meaningful and accessible, based on personal interests and capabilities. Adequate skill and fitness levels provide a basis for continued learning and participation. Students should develop an awareness of how and why adult patterns of participation change throughout their life and should be prepared with meaningful strategies to deal with those changes.

The emphasis for the twelfth grade will be to:

* Have the skills, knowledge, interest, and desire to independently maintain an active lifestyle throughout their life.

* Understand how activity participation patterns are likely to change throughout life and have some strategies to deal with those changes.

Sample Benchmarks:

1. Participates regularly in physical activities that contribute to the attainment of and maintenance of personal physical activity goals.
2. Willingly participates in games, sports, dance, outdoor pursuits, and other physical activities that contribute to the attainment of personal goals and the maintenance of wellness.
3. Identifies the effects of age, gender, race, ethnicity, socioeconomic status, and culture upon physical activity preferences and participation.
4. Understands the ways in which personal characteristics, performance styles, and activity preferences will change over the life span.
5. Feels empowered to maintain and improve physical fitness, motor skills, and knowledge about physical activity.

Assessment Examples:

1. Student journal

Students will keep a journal reporting weekly participation in a personal physical activity plan for a minimum of 2 months. They should describe the process and conditions which limited or enhanced their participation in physical activity during the previous week. Moreover, the students will write a summary of the 2-month experience, including: (1) conditions that most commonly limited their participation and (2) suggestions of realistic changes that could be made in their lifestyle to attain a level of participation that would be health-enhancing and help them achieve their personal activity goals.

Criteria for Assessment:
a. Maintains journal over a period of 3 months
b. Describes conditions and suggestions realistically and fully

2. Interview

Students are requested to interview a man and a woman from each of the following age ranges, 10 to 30 years, 40 to 50 years, and 65 to 75 years. They should determine the physical activity patterns for each individual and then evaluate these activity patterns to determine if each person is taking advantage of the physiological, psychological, and social benefits of physical activity. In addition, evaluate the activity for possible gender or age-related trends. Lastly, for each person, make suggestions as to how they can adjust their activity regimen to maximize the healthful benefits of the activity.

Criteria for Assessment:
a. Interviews are completed
b. Describes activity patterns accurately
c. Suggests appropriate activity
d. Analyzes gender-related activity patterns correctly

3. Student Project

Students shall seek and participate in a series of physical activity episodes of personal interest involving skill and fitness improvement or maintenance. They are then requested to prepare a scrapbook or journal that provides evidence of personal goals, achievements, and quality of participation.

Criteria for Assessment:
a. Provides evidence of personal goals
b. Includes appropriate experiences to meet the personal activity goals

4. Student project

Students select a physical activity based on their own personal interest, desire, and capability. Then students develop a plan for implementing a regular program involving this physical activity in which they will describe the skill and fitness development of the activity, describe practice sessions, equipment, facilities, instruction (if necessary) and cost. After several weeks of actual participation in the planned program, students will write a summary indicating how they felt about the program. The summary will include a statement indicating level of goal fulfillment, enjoyment, and potential for long-term involvement.

Criteria for Assessment:
a. Incorporates goals for the development of skill and fitness in their plan
b. Accurately describes appropriate practice sessions, equipment, cost, and instruction
c. Includes personal perspectives, goal attainment, and analysis of long-term participation

4. Achieves and maintains a health-enhancing level of physical fitness.

The student at this level should be totally independent in assessing, achieving, and maintaining personal health-related fitness goals and should be motivated to do so. Utilizing basic principles of training, students are now able to design personal fitness programs that encompass all components of fitness. Ongoing attention to their health-related fitness status should be a way of life for students, as they assume adult role responsibilities to participate in physical activity on a regular basis.

The emphasis for the twelfth grade student will be to:

- Participate regularly in health-enhancing fitness activities independent of teaching mandates.

- Demonstrate the skill, knowledge, and desire to monitor and adjust activity levels to meet personal fitness needs.

- Design a personal fitness program.

- Meet the health-related fitness standards as defined by Fitnessgram.

Sample Benchmarks:

1. Monitors exercise and other behaviors related to health-related fitness.
2. Maintains appropriate levels of cardiovascular and respiratory efficiency, muscular strength and endurance, flexibility, and body composition necessary for a healthful lifestyle.
3. Uses the results of fitness assessments to guide changes in his or her personal program of physical activity.

Assessment Examples:

1. Student project

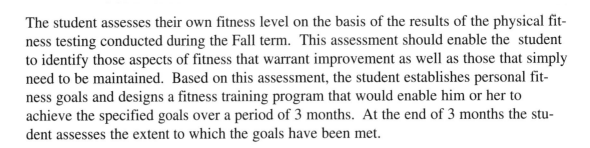
The student assesses their own fitness level on the basis of the results of the physical fitness testing conducted during the Fall term. This assessment should enable the student to identify those aspects of fitness that warrant improvement as well as those that simply need to be maintained. Based on this assessment, the student establishes personal fitness goals and designs a fitness training program that would enable him or her to achieve the specified goals over a period of 3 months. At the end of 3 months the student assesses the extent to which the goals have been met.

Criteria for Assessment:
a. Assessment of their current level of fitness is accurate
b. Establishes realistic, yet challenging goals
c. Designs a program that has the potential to meet the identified goals
d. Accurately assesses the degree to which the goals have been attained
e. Meets personal goals as established

2. Formal test

The student participates in the Fitnessgram Physical Fitness Test and meets the criteria established for their age and gender.

3. Student project

In order to analyze one's diet, the student keeps a 3-day record (or it could be for a longer period) of everything they eat. This record must include the type of food eaten as well as the quantity. At the end of each day the nutrient value (calories, fat, protein, cholesterol, minerals) for the foods eaten is determined using appropriate nutritive value charts. Alternatively, the use of a computerized dietary analysis program greatly simplifies this process. After the 3-day period, an average for the 3 days is computed for each nutrient and these values are compared to the Recommended Dietary Allowances (RDA). The student then prepares a written self-assessment of their diet.

Criteria for Assessment:
a. Maintains dietary record accurately
b. Accurately determines the nutrient value of foods eaten
c. Self-assessment is appropriate given the dietary analysis completed
d. Uses the dietary analysis to accurately assess their personal eating habits

4. Portfolio

The student develops a personal portfolio containing: (1) reports of his or her own health-related fitness status over a period of at least 1 year, (2) personal fitness goals and a discussion of the extent to which they have met at the end of the year, (3) records of physical activity, nutritional habits, and other behaviors that might affect one's physical fitness, and (4) an assessment of one's personal fitness level at the end of the year and a discussion of what behavior modifications are needed to maintain satisfactory aspects of fitness or improve those aspects that are presently below desired goals.

Criteria for Assessment:
a. Portfolio contains all of the required elements
b. Presents sufficient documentation to support the fitness profile presented
c. Correctly assesses their personal fitness level and associates present status to documented behavior
d. Demonstrates understanding of the behavior, knowledge and skills needed to maintain or modify their existing fitness level.

5. Student report

Students are asked to prepare a report that discusses their physical activity plans in the near-future following their graduation. In addition, the report discusses what plans the student has for maintaining a satisfactory level of physical fitness 10 years after graduation and what barriers are likely to be faced in attempting to maintain this level of fitness.

Criteria for Assessment:
a. Cites realistic physical activity expectations immediately after graduation as well as 10 years later
b. Correctly identifies barriers to regular exercise likely to be encountered following graduation from high school
c. Logically organizes and writes report in a style commensurate with the expectations of a twelfth grade student

5. Demonstrates responsible personal and social behavior in physical activity settings

Twelfth grade students demonstrate the ability to initiate responsible behavior, function independently, and positively influence the behavior of others in physical activity settings. They demonstrate leadership by holding themselves and others responsible for following safe practices, rules, procedures, and etiquette in all physical activity settings. They act as a neutralizer in avoiding conflict or as a mediator in settling conflicts.

The emphasis for the twelfth grade student will be to:

• Initiate independent and responsible personal behavior in physical activity settings.

• Accept the responsibility for taking a leadership role and willingly follow as appropriate in order to accomplish group goals.

• Anticipate potentially dangerous consequences and outcomes of participation in physical activity.

Sample Benchmarks:

1. Sets personal goals for activity and works toward their achievement.
2. Encourages others to apply appropriate etiquette in all physical activity settings.
3. Responds to inflammatory situations with mature personal control.
4. Diffuses potential conflicts by communicating with other participants.
5. Creates a safe environment for their own skill practice.
6. Takes a supportive role in an activity.
7. Cheers outstanding performances of opponents as well as the "favored" team.

Assessment Examples:

1. Teacher observation - observational record

Students participate in a ropes course activity unit in which they are asked to work together to accomplish group goals. At the completion of each day on the course, the teacher, based upon their observation of student performance, records information for each student concerning the extent to which that student contributed to the group goals for that day. Each student is likewise asked to rate their own participation.

Criteria for Assessment:
a. Assumes an active leader role, a supportive follower role, and a passive follower role as appropriate
b. Contributes to the group process by maintaining a balance between leader and follower roles

2. Teacher observation - observational record

Students are encouraged to accept the responsibility for independent work toward the development of personal objectives during a physical education class unit. The teacher takes 1 minute during each class period to observe student behavior and do a "workcheck" of what students are doing during the independent work part of the class period.

Criteria for Assessment:
a. Works independently
b. Works productively and at a high level of engagement
c. Demonstrates responsible behavior that is not disruptive to others

3. Student report

Students are asked to observe a peer mediation session. Based upon their observation, students prepare a report describing the incident that led to the mediation and discuss their reactions to the mediation session. In addition, students should propose possible solutions to the problem.

Criteria for Assessment:
a. Correctly describes the events leading to the mediation session

b. Recognizes probable factors that led to the dispute
c. Makes appropriate recommendations that are likely to have positive results
d. Demonstrates an understanding of the importance of mediation as a way of resolving disputes

6. Demonstrates understanding and respect for differences among people in physical activity settings

The focus in the twelfth grade is on culminating experiences that indicate the student's ability to synthesize and evaluate knowledge regarding the role of physical activity in a culturally diverse society. Emphasis is placed on the influence of age, disability, gender, race, ethnicity, socioeconomic status, and culture on making enlightened personal choices for engaging in physical activity over the life span. In addition, students develop strategies for inclusion of others in physical activity.

The emphasis for the twelfth grade student will be to:

*   Recognize the influence of participation in physical activity on fostering appreciation of cultural, ethnic, gender, and physical diversity.

*   Develop strategies for including persons from diverse backgrounds and characteristics in physical activity they select for leisure pursuits.

Sample Benchmarks:

1. Identifies the effects of age, gender, race, ethnicity, socioeconomic status, and culture upon physical activity preferences and participation.
2. Displays a willingness to experiment with the sport and activity of other cultures.
3. Develops strategies for including persons of diverse backgrounds and abilities in physical activity.

Assessment Examples:

1. Student report

The types of physical activities and the time spent participating in physical activity changes over the life span. Several factors such as age, gender, socioeconomic status, and cultural background affect the choices one makes as activity patterns change. Students are asked to prepare a report discussing how these factors effect one's choice of physical activities in young adulthood, middle age, and old age?

Criteria for Assessment:
a. Identifies factors associated with the various age groups discussed
b. Notes how these factors influence sport and activity participation
c. Identifies the importance of geographical area as background for the factors listed in the task

2. Group project

Students are requested to organize and conduct a sport or game adapted for physically challenged individuals. Invite nondisabled individuals to participate with the purpose of gaining insights into the challenges that person's with disabilities face while participating in physical activity. Interview participants after the activity and report (orally or in writing) insights relative to the experience.

Criteria for Assessment:
a. Identifies an appropriate activity and adaptations for persons with a disability
b. Displays a sensitivity to the diverse skill levels and backgrounds of participants
c. Organizes and reports the interview material in such a way that demonstrates an in-depth treatment of the topic
d. Identifies personal knowledge acquired as a result of the experience

3. Student project

Students are asked to gather a list of the various professional, college, and high school mascots (both picture and name) and identify which might be offensive for different cultural, ethnic, and gender groups. Reasons for the unpleasantness are identified.

Criteria for Assessment:
a. Compiles a comprehensive list of mascots
b. Correctly identifies the troublesome mascots and the group(s) that might find them offensive
c. Provides sound reasons for the offensiveness of the identified mascots

4. Student project

Students are requested to research physical activity options available within their community and to select and design a physical activity program for themselves that emphasizes multicultural awareness and cross-cultural experiences.

Criteria for Assessment:
a. Identifies appropriate activities
b. Articulates the contributions of each selected activity to multicultural awareness

7. Understands that physical activity provides the opportunity for enjoyment, challenge, self-expression, and social interaction.

The twelfth grade student enjoys selected activities in which he or she regularly participates, alone or with friends. Competitive, recreational, and social situations can all provide feelings of challenge. The student is readily able to express several reasons why participation in these activities is enjoyable and desirable.

The emphasis for the twelfth grade student will be to:

• Enjoy regular participation in physical activity.

• Recognize that physical activity can provide opportunities for positive social interaction.

- Enjoy learning new activities.

- Recognize the positive feelings that result from physical activity participation alone and with others.

Sample Benchmarks:

1. Derives genuine pleasure from participating in physical activity.
2. Enters competition or activity voluntarily.

Assessment Examples:

1. Student project

Students are asked to assume that they are the recreation director for a camp or inner city school project designed to help youngsters. They must design a program and choose activities for a week that will provide challenge and enjoyment for all participants.

Criteria for Assessment:
a. Identifies a variety of activities that can provide enjoyment for the participants
b. Identifies aspects of the activities that are enjoyable
c. Designs a program that reflects balance in terms of activity

2. Portfolio

Students are requested to develop a portfolio that documents their participation in a physical activity (sport, dance or nontraditional activity). Furthermore, students shall maintain a log of their participation and record in a journal their feelings following competition or participation in the selected activity. Additional pamphlets or material will be used to supplement the portfolio.

Criteria for Assessment:
a. Accurately records participation
b. Identifies feelings of enjoyment, success, and challenge as reasons for participation
c. Identifies negative feelings that may surround events during participation
d. Participates in the activity on a regular basis

3. Event task

Students sign up for a Big Sister/Big Brother program with a friend. An activity is selected that can be done with the "little brother or sister." With their peer, teach this person how to play or participate in the selected activity (e.g., increase their skill, make it more challenging). The activity may be one in which the student has limited experience, that will require asking others for help or going to the library for additional information. Students shall maintain a log of this experience and record their feelings of teaching and sharing the activity with someone else. Also note the reaction that the "little brother or sister" has to the activity.

Criteria for Assessment:
a. Enjoys sharing the activity with others
b. Looks forward and anticipates the time spent in this task
c. Enjoys the social interaction gained in this experience
d. Articulates personal feelings associated with teaching or sharing the chosen activity
e. Recognizes reaction of "little brother or sister" to the experience

4. Student project

Students will make a list of all of the activities they have participated in over the years and rank-order these activities in terms of personal preference. Group the activities into the following categories: most preferred, somewhat preferred and least preferred. Students are requested to review the activity groupings to determine similarities and differences between activities in each group. A written report is prepared describing the basis for the activity groupings as well as an interpretation of what this information may mean regarding their preferences for physical activity participation.

Criteria for Assessment:
a. Accurately lists and groups activities
b. Appropriately identifies similarities and differences between activities
c. Identifies basis for grouping the activities as they have
d. Demonstrates insight into own preferences for activity

Appendixes

Appendix A: Assessment

Section 1. Overview

Two cornerstones of the current educational reform movement are accountability and assessment. Accountability refers to the responsibility of teachers for effective teaching and hence, to a certain degree, for student learning. Assessment refers to the process of testing and evaluating students to determine progress towards program goals.

Traditionally, the assessment model advocated for physical education involves
- formally stating the objectives of instruction (typically knowledge, psychomotor, and psycho-social objectives)
- preassessing students
- measuring achievement of objectives using valid and reliable tests during and after delivery of appropriate instructional activities
- evaluating student progress towards meeting the stated objectives in a formative framework using a criterion-referenced grading system.

Three primary principles underlay the traditional model of assessment (Wood, in press):

- **Establish appropriate instructional objectives.** Objectives for physical education can be found at the national, state, and local levels. The NASPE *Content Standards and Assessment Guide for School Physical Education* represents the most recent national standards for physical education. These standards reflect what a physically educated student should know and be able to do at each grade level. Rather than defining curriculum, these standards provide signposts for teachers and program accountability; although educators will find the standards useful in designing appropriate physical education curricula.
- **Use of appropriate tests to measure characteristics related to instructional objectives.** Assessment can take many forms. Informal assessment is used to enhance day-to-day instruction. It is usually nongraded, nonrecorded, and can range from simple observation of student performance and verbal checking for student understanding to nongraded pop quizzes. In contrast, formal assessment is used for gathering evidence to be used in formulating student grades, program evaluation, developing and revising program objectives, and for providing feedback for students. Formal assessment involves the administration of valid (tests that measure what they are supposed to measure) and reliable (measurement that is relatively error-free) assessment tools to evaluate the extent to which students have met the objectives of the program (see Section 2 below). The degree to which tests should be valid and reliable is in direct proportion to the importance of the decisions made based on test scores. For example, if sport skills tests are to account for 75 percent of the grade in physical education, the test should be chosen or developed with careful attention paid to validity and reliability. Traditionally, formal assessment has involved the use of sport skills tests, motor performance checklists and rating scales, knowledge tests, and subjective measures of psychosocial development. More recently; however, a number of alternative assessment strategies such as authentic assessment, and performance assessment are gaining

in popularity (see Section 3 below). The NASPE *Content Standards and Assessment Guide for School Physical Education* includes many assessment options and examples with each content standard. In addition, Section 4 below provides more detailed descriptions of assessment options used in the document. However, it must be emphasized that these options are only a sample of a broader range of available assessment tools. Detailed descriptions of how to develop valid and reliable checklists and rating scales, sport skills tests, and knowledge tests can be found in texts such as Safrit and Wood (1995) and Baumgartner and Jackson (1995). Other useful resources (see Appendix B) are Strand and Wilson (1993); Collins and Hodges (1978); Hensley, Morrow, and East (1990); McGee and Farrow (1987); and Schick (1981).

- **Development of an evaluation scheme that reflects attainment of the instructional objectives.** Grades in physical education should reflect attainment of stated instructional objectives. A teacher's grading plan should be a reflection of both the teacher's choice of objectives and the importance given to each objective. If a program emphasizes knowledge of physical fitness principles, performance in selected sports or dance and multicultural awareness, then the grading scheme should reflect each of those elements.

Section 2. Measurement Concepts

Two desirable characteristics of tests are validity and reliability. Validity refers to the appropriateness of test score interpretation, while reliability refers to test scores that are replicable or relatively free from error. The degree to which a test is valid and reliable reflects the degree of confidence that the test scores provide credible evidence regarding student performance.

The methodology for determining evidence for validity and reliability is diverse and ranges from logical analyses to complex statistical computations. For the public school physical education setting; however, a number of relatively easy methods provide adequate evidence. In addition, the degree to which tests should be valid and reliable is in direct proportion to the importance of the decisions made based on test scores.

<u>**Content-Related Evidence for Validity.**</u>   For most tests the first steps in test development are (a) explicitly defining the student attributes to be measured (determined in relation to the instructional objectives) and (b) designing a test to measure the important attributes. If it can be shown that the attributes measured by the test reflect those attributes defined in step (a) then evidence has been presented for content validity. For traditional written tests (e.g., multiple choice tests) a table of specifications or blueprint that outlines the content to be covered by the test and the level of cognition (e.g., memorization, understanding and application of knowledge) required by students can be developed. Test questions are then written to reflect the content and behaviors outlined in the table of specifications. Content-related evidence for validity is assessed by matching the test questions to the table of specifications. If the test questions reflect the table of specifications then content validity is achieved. A similar process known as logical validity (Safrit and Wood, 1995) can be employed for tests of motor performance (e.g., a test of the tennis serve):

- The important elements of skill are listed.
- A test is constructed to measure the important elements of skill
- The test is scored such that higher scores reflect more proficient performance in the

defined elements
  • If the elements examined by the test match the important elements outlined in the test purpose, a claim can be made for logical validity.

Reflection on the process of determining evidence for content-validity reveals that test construction is a systematic and goal directed process and not simply a matter of haphazardly developing test questions or elements. Achieving a valid test requires knowledge of the instructional objectives, contemplation of the important content and behaviors to be examined, careful construction of test questions and elements and examination of the degree to which the test questions and elements reflect the important content and behaviors.

Criterion-Related Evidence for Validity. While content-related evidence for validity is an appropriate starting point in the validation process, for some types of tests, most notably motor performance tests, additional evidence for validity can easily be determined. Criterion-related evidence for validity compares test scores with another test (the criterion) considered to be a better, although often less practical or feasible measure of the characteristic. For example, after determining the logical validity of a tennis serve test, a teacher administers the test to 30 students in his or her class. In addition, the school's tennis coach is asked to independently evaluate each student on their tennis serve. The coach's rating is the criterion or "gold standard" against which the field test is compared. Criterion-related evidence for validity is indicated if students who score well on the tennis serve test are also rated highly in tennis serving skill by the coach and if students who score low on the serve test are rated as less skilled in serving by the coach. A common method for quantifying this type of relationship is by computing the correlation coefficient between the tennis serve test scores and the coach's rating of each student. Correlation above 0.80 are acceptable for most purposes in a school setting (Safrit and Wood, 1995), although the acceptable magnitude depends in large part on the uses of the test scores.

Reliability. Reliability refers to the consistency of test scores over repeated testing or the relative freedom of scores from error. In physical education settings two types of evidence for reliability are important: *test-retest reliability* and *objectivity*. Test-retest reliability is the consistency of scores over time. That is, if you administer a test to students today and measure the same students using the same methods two days from now, the same scores should be obtained. Objectivity or rater reliability refers to the degree of consistency of scores when two different raters or the same rater on two occasions scores a group of students. Objectivity is a significant issue when scoring essay tests and written projects, observational instruments such as checklists and rating scales, and alternative assessments such as portfolios and event tasks. Clearly defined scoring criteria and significant practice using a scoring system lead to greater objectivity when using such assessments.

Section 3. Alternative Assessment

Traditionally, assessment specialists have advocated the use of standardized tests for assessing physical fitness, sport skills, knowledge, and psychosocial characteristics. Such tests have a high degree of validity and reliability and are accompanied by tables of norms or criterion-referenced standards. From the practitioner's point of view, however, such tests tend to be impractical and often fail to measure the instructional objectives of interest to teachers. Riding the current wave of educational reform with its emphasis on outcomes based education, integrated learning, and critical thinking skills, a number of alternative assessment strategies have captured the attention of teachers and administrators, eager to develop accountability systems to serve both the needs of students in a changing world and the demands of parents for responsibility in the classroom.

Alternative assessment can take many forms such as portfolios, discussions and debates, event tasks, case studies, student logs, and role playing. Such assessments are characterized by the following:

- tasks that directly examine the behavior the teacher wishes to measure
- a focus on product and quality of performance
- criterion-referenced scoring
- assessment of higher levels of learning
- student participation in development of the assessment and ownership of the final product
- assessment criteria that are given to students in advance (Bartz, Anderson-Robinson, & Hillman, 1994).

Rubrics are the scoring criteria by which student performance is judged. They are used most often with alternative assessments such as portfolios, event tasks, and student performance but can actually be used for other types of assessment as well. They are written by the teacher before instruction begins and shared with students as the unit or project is explained. Because students have the criteria very early, they have a standard by which they can judge their own performance, thus providing feedback during instruction.

When writing a rubric (see the following sample rubric), all important criteria should be addressed. If teachers are evaluating a project with several components, they may choose to write a single scoring rubric that addresses all the components (holistic rubric) or several rubrics to address each topic or goal (analytic rubric). Although the former is easier to score, the reliability is generally better with the latter. Either format is acceptable.

Start by writing down the components for the top level. There are different philosophies concerning the top level. One method is to write the ideal or optimal criteria so that very few, maybe only 1% or 2%, of your students will ever reach this. The reasoning behind this is that students will not have a ceiling effect and can always be striving to make their best better. Alternatively, write the top criteria at a level that better or "A" students would be able to achieve.

Most alternative assessments use rubrics with four to six levels. Each level is somewhat easier to achieve than the previous level as the standards are lower. The teacher must also decide what is the least acceptable level of performance. The levels of the rubric should be graduated between the upper and lower level.

Scoring Rubrics
Example of a scoring rubric:

Score 4 points if the student:
- Follows all directions and finishes all parts of the question
- Clearly answers the question so that others can understand
- Demonstrates that he or she really understands the information that is asked about and is not just giving related facts. In other words, the information is applied in some manner.
- Answers the question concisely, giving the best way to solve the problem presented
- Can apply the knowledge by showing connections between ideas and the real world, by comparing different ideas, and showing how the ideas work together

Score 3 points if the student:
- Follows the directions and finishes most of the parts of the question
- Clearly answers the question so that others can understand
- Demonstrates an understanding of the "big picture" related to the question but there may be a few little mistakes or wrong ideas

Score 2 points if the student:
- Follows some of the directions and finishes some parts of the question

- Answers the question clearly so that others can understand, but the answer may not be complete
- Demonstrates only a partial understanding of the knowledge and concepts necessary to complete the question

Score 1 point if the student:
- Understands only a small part of the information asked for in the question
- Answers only a small part of the question

Score 0 points if the student:
- Answers the question completely wrong or has nothing to do with the question

Blank
- Student did not give any answer at all

The level at which the rubric is written will depend upon several things;e.g., the length of time spent on the unit; age and ability level of student; amount of equipment available. Also, some of these assessments can be used for multiple purposes, depending on the teacher's goals. A teacher should start with a list of goals and concepts that students should know and then give lesser points for answers that are not complete or do not meet teacher expectations.

Alternative assessment is labeled "authentic" when the tasks are conducted in real-to- life contexts (Meyer, 1992). For example, to assess student learning in a physical fitness unit, traditional assessment involving written tests of knowledge and understanding or projects such as essays can be delivered. In contrast, an alternative assessment might consist of a group project to (a) assess the fitness needs of teachers and staff at the school, (b) design a custom physical fitness program for these individuals, (c) provide instruction on how to safely and effectively participate in fitness activities, and (d) monitor the individuals as they progress through the program. The teacher assumes the role of a facilitator to help students formulate appropriate questions and as a guide to finding appropriate answers. At each stage of the process, students present written and/or oral synopses and reflections of their challenges and successes, culminating in a portfolio that reflects both the products and process of student learning. Moreover, unlike more traditional types of assessment, feedback is given to students during the process so that learning takes place during the assessment. This type of assessment can be described as "alternative" to more traditional forms of assessment and as "authentic" because it assesses performance in a real-to-life rather than a contrived context.

The NASPE *Content Standards and Assessment Guide for School Physical Education* focuses on alternative assessment options because these types of assessment devices are not as common or as well articulated in physical education settings. This should not be interpreted as a condemnation of more traditional assessment devices. A balanced assessment strategy should employ assessment devices that best assess the instructional objectives of the physical education program.

From a measurement perspective, constructing and administering valid and reliable alternative assessments is a challenging task. Issues that require careful consideration include the following(Pierson and Beck, 1993):

- Are the tasks worthy of being assessed?
- How well do the tasks provided by the assessment match the proficiencies to be assessed (i.e., do the tasks measure what they are supposed to measure)?
- Is the end product clearly defined?
- Do the scoring rubrics, guidelines, or procedures accurately reflect the agreed-upon proficiencies?
- Are the criteria for administering and scoring the test precise and clear?
- Are the scoring rubrics precise enough to achieve a degree of inter-rater reliability?

- How will the assessment results be used (i.e., grading, improving instructional practices)?

Because many alternative assessments require elements of critical thinking, problem solving, and writing competency, developers of such tests should be aware of issues such as linguistic appropriateness and fairness or "opportunity to learn" so that some students are not disadvantaged by learning disabilities, lack of facilities or equipment, or language barriers (Baker, 1994). In addition, alternative assessment often requires teachers to critically analyze student work, a task for which teachers often are not trained and do not have time. Moreover, performance assessments can involve long-term group and individual projects that may require that teachers assume the role of facilitator rather than of instructor.

Alternative assessments provide an exciting assessment option for physical educators. Worthen (1993) provides 10 conditions important to a school's readiness to implement alternative assessment strategies:

- Desire for better assessment information.
- Indications that current assessment is creating negative side effects.
- Staff openness to innovations.
- Conceptual clarity about alternative assessment and its advantages and disadvantages.
- Assessment literacy.
- Clarity about desired student outcomes.
- Content or curricula ill-suited to traditional tests.
- School examples of alternative assessment.
- Willingness to critique assessment methods.
- Patron's and policy maker's openness to new forms of assessments.

The NASPE *Content Standards and Assessment Guide for School Physical Education* can assist schools with defining appropriate outcomes and providing examples of alternative assessments. NASPE invites you and your school to use this document as a springboard for maximizing the effectiveness of assessing physical education learning outcomes.

Section 4. Assessment Options

Some of the assessment options described in this document may not be familiar to readers. To assist those interested in using various assessment options, the following descriptions, examples, and hints for effective use are presented:

STUDENT PROJECT

Definition/Description:

Students engage in building a scenario, determining goals, planning a program of participation to achieve outcomes, and implementing the plan to the completion of the goals. Student projects provide for a range of strategies and results including the following: the application of the processes of data collection, goal setting, planning, analysis, decision making, problem-solving; development and application of skill and knowledge to real-life situations to solve problems or create "new" interventions to reach personal goals; may include multiple objectives or outcomes; combine multiple assessment options (logs, journals, reports); student autonomy in choosing procedures and reaching conclusions; solo or multiple students; multiple resources; changes in status, behaviors, conditions; authenticity; performance products; flexibility of time (complexity of task determines time); and, integration of multiple content areas, concepts, and applications.

Projects are assigned at the beginning of student learning sequences (units, courses) and are integrated with instruction. Criteria for assessment projects are presented at the initiation of the assignment.

Example: (Suggested Application: Grade Levels 10, 12
Standards #1, 2, 3, 4, 5, 6, 7)

Student analyzes interests, desires, capabilities and commitment for engaging in a physical activity of his or her choice. Using personal data about health and motor fitness status, create a plan for developing skills and fitness necessary for participation in a series of episodes in the chosen activity. Include a plan for skill improvement, practice, fitness conditioning, securing equipment, time, facilities, instruction, finances, and other people with whom to participate. The teacher may be used as a resource for planning and locating appropriate opportunities for participation. The project may be used to assess achievement of several other outcomes. The student will provide the following evidence of completion: a videotape of one episode in the series; a log of participation throughout the series; a written summary of the experience reflecting feelings about success, benefits, enjoyment , and potential for lifelong participation.

Criteria for Assessment:
1. Analyzes personal fitness status to plan skill and fitness development.
2. Applies basic skills and movement concepts to perform proficiently and creatively.
3. Applies principles of training to improve skill and fitness.
4. Uses resources to solve problems that enhance or limit participation.
5. Reflects on the benefits, enjoyment, and challenges that result from participation in physical activity.

Scoring:
- Exemplary: Successfully completes the series of episodes, demonstrating synthesis of skill, knowledge and attitudes to plan and perform proficiently and creatively, and assumes all the responsibilities of reporting the results.
- Acceptable: Completes the series of episodes, demonstrating application of skills, concepts and attitudes to perform basic skills with competence required for the pleasurable performance and assumes all the responsibilities of reporting the results.
- Needs Improvement: Planning, participation, and reporting reflect insufficient skill and knowledge.
- Unacceptable: Planning, participation, and reporting are incomplete.

Report Form:
- Checklist of multiple forms
- Written participation plan
- Records of fitness assessment (health and motor)
- Log of participation
- Videotape of performance
- Summary report

Hints for Development and Use:

- Experience with a variety of teaching styles will increase the successful direction and completion of student projects.
- Small projects that give students increasing amounts of responsibility for their own learning should be given in the early grades to prepare them for the complexity of this assessment.
- Criteria for assessment and scoring procedures are explained to the student at the beginning of the project.
- Multiple scorers that include community experts, cross-disciplinary, and multiple grade levels might be used.

- Pilot field testing of this option should be completed before results of this assessment are used for purposes of promotion or graduation.
- Student projects permit a high degree of individuality.
- Scoring rubrics will be necessary for each component of the project.
- Before assigning projects, evidence should be available which indicates mastery of basic concepts and skills necessary for successful completion.
- The element of choice provided by projects enables acceptance of learning of essential skills, concepts, and practices in a way that is important to the student.

STUDENT LOG

Definition/Description:

Students record performance of specific behaviors over a period of time that identifies products, time intervals, decisions/choices, and reflections. Recorded items should indicate critical factors relative to expected results. Information may show performance changes, sequence of behaviors, choices, feelings, documentation of conditions, progress, process, and/or regularity of participation. Logs may be kept by individual students, small groups, or whole classes. Information can be used to justify program change, make predictions, and in combination with other assessment options.

Example: (Suggested application: Grade Levels 2, 4, 6
Standard #3)

Students are asked to share their involvement in physical activities during nonschool times. Entries are made on a collective class wall chart to indicate what, when, and where activities are performed and the number of students who participated. Anecdotal records are made by the teacher for individual students indicating what influences the student's participation including the level of success/enjoyment expressed, student likes or dislikes, involvement with family and friends.

WALL CHART:

DATE	ACTIVITY	# OF PARTICIPANTS	WHERE	TIME	COMMENTS:
4/1	Rope jump	6	Yard	30 min	Double Dutch I don't like when the rope is too fast

Criteria for Assessment:
1. Activities selected have potential for vigorous physical activity.
2. Students use available opportunities to be involved in physical activity at least three times a week.

Scoring:
- Exemplary: Participates more than three times a week
- Acceptable: Participates at least three times a week
- Needs Improvement: Participates less than three times a week
- Unacceptable: No participation in vigorous activity

Report Form: Oral report to teacher

Hints for Development and Use:

- Critical factors about information to be collected determine the data to be recorded on the log.
- Reporting forms must be simple for quick recording.
- Data collected provides information that may be used for other assessment options or instructional strategies (e.g., learning curve).
- Keeping a log is a motivational tool.
- A log provides a tangible record of progress for both the student and the teacher.
- Individual logs promote student responsibility for personal learning.

STUDENT JOURNAL

Definition/Description:

Student record of participation, results, responses to, feelings, perceptions, or reflections about actual happenings or results. Entries, made at regular intervals over time, may serve as indicators of success, failure, benefits, or other intangible products of participation. Entries are not viewed as right or wrong since they are reflections about personal performance including social and psychological perspectives. Students may describe both positive and negative behavior. Journal entries are used to summarize, compare and contrast like and unlike experiences, provide opportunity for self-analysis of personal meaning and quality of participation, record behavior adjustments, compare results of other assessment options including conditions which contribute, enhance, or limit participation, and as a resource of suggestions for change. Journal entries can be reviewed to determine how a student processes both internal and external information about his or her performance.

Example: (Suggested Application: Grade Level 10
Standard # 7)

During an adventure education experience (i.e., ropes course, climbing a wall, nature hikes, camping, canoeing), record in a journal the feelings and thoughts experienced throughout.

Criteria for Assessment:
1. Analyzes and expresses feelings about physical activity.
2. Identifies evidence of success, challenge, and enjoyment present in the activity.
3. Explains challenge that adventure activities provide.
4. Describes the positive effects friends and companions bring to this experience.

Scoring:
- Exemplary: Expresses feelings of personal participation and in sharing it with friends.
- Acceptable: Identifies feelings of personal participation
- Needs improvement: Has difficult expressing feelings about participation.
- Unacceptable: Does not make journal entries.

Reporting Form: Composition notebook

Hints for Development and Use:

- Writing should be used in simple episodes at first.
- Writings should not be judged as right or wrong.
- Student writings should be protected as private information to be shared only by the student or with student permission.

- Students might be given a choice to determine who may read the journal.
- Students may be asked to use the criteria for assessment to summarize the journal for scoring and reporting purposes.
- Summary reports might be used as an interdisciplinary assessment including communication arts and social studies.

PARENTAL REPORT

Definition/Description:

Record of student regularity, progress, process or product of participation that has been verified by the parent(s). The report may include verification by signature of a student's recorded report or by anecdotal comments of the parent or person who has observed the out-of-class performance.

Example: (Suggested application: Grade Level K, 2
Standard #3)

An anecdotal record is kept of observations over a period of time about the physical activities of children while under the supervision of parents or guardians and during nonschool time. The report should include play choices, purposeful practice, formal activities (sports clubs, dance lessons), or family activities. The report may be in the form of a log or a journal.

Criteria for Assessment:
1. Participates in a variety of physical activities.
2. Participates in health-enhancing activities regularly.

Scoring:
- Exemplary: Participates in a variety of activities more than three times per week.
- Acceptable: Participates in health-enhancing activities at least three times a week.
- Needs improvement: Participates in health enhancing physical activities less than three times a week.
- Unacceptable: Does not participate in physical activities outside of the school program.

Reporting Form:
(NAME OF SCHOOL)
PHYSICAL EDUCATION - PARENTAL REPORT FORM

Student Name_____

Parent Name_____

Describe the involvement of the student named above in physical activities each day during the week of _____. Include formal/informal, family/individual activities, the length of time spent, and any comments that indicate the level of performance.

_____

_____

_____

_____

_____

<u>**Hints for Development and Use:**</u>

• Directions for parents should be written and reviewed by a small group of parents before involving parents of all students.
• Results may indicate special individual needs, weaknesses, or interests.
• Results may indicate parents with special interests that may be a useful resource.
• Results may indicate a need for instructional emphasis to enhance special community interests that are attractive to students.
• Parental involvement may help to stimulate more interest in planning physical activities in which the whole family can participate.

INTERVIEW

<u>**Definition/Description:**</u>

One-to-one discussion with a planned sequence of questions to obtain information (e.g., cognitive, affective, statistical). Most often thought of as teacher-to-student interviews for the purposes of obtaining information on student thoughts, feelings, and understandings. However, student-to-student or student-to-persons in the community interviews may be used for such purposes as analyzing activity patterns or computing frequency of exercise.

<u>**Example:**</u>

Interview two persons from each of the following age groups: 20 to 30 years, 40 to 50 years, 65+ years. Plan your interview questions in order to determine the physical activity for each individual. Use the information obtained from the interview to evaluate physical activity patterns to determine if each person is taking advantage of the physiological, psychological, and social benefits of physical activity.

<u>**Hints for Development and Use:**</u>

• Questions for the interview should be planned and sequential.
• The interview should be planned with a clear purpose in mind.
• Teacher-to-student interviews offer excellent opportunities for encouragement as well as for feedback information.
• When asking questions of students, be patient in waiting for the student to articulate his or her response.
• Remember, the purpose of the interview is to obtain information, not to impose your opinions.
• Student-to-others interviews are usually for obtaining information. Teacher-to-student interviews provide insight into the student's personal feelings, perceptions of strengths as well as student comprehension.

PEER OBSERVATION

<u>**Definition/Description:**</u>

The observation of students by other students to assess competence in performance of skill and demonstration of selected critical elements of skill. It is most often used for the observation of critical elements that lead to a mature execution of a particular skill. Informal peer observation is used throughout teaching to help students evaluate progress toward the goal (e.g., inclusion of all components for a gymnastics routine or creative dance, correct pathway of travel in response

to task). Peer observation feedback includes verbal discussion, verbal response, thumbs up or thumbs down, and written feedback. Videotape is a helpful support technology for peer observation.

Example:

Students observe for critical elements in the preparatory phase of a designated skill. For example, student "A" throws a ball toward a target five times using the overhand throw. Student "B" (the observer) focuses on the critical element stated by the teacher as the focus of the exercise (e.g., opposite foot forward, side to the target). the peer observer signals thumbs up if the critical element is correctly executed.

Hints for Development and Use:

- Criteria for assessment must be clear to the observer (i.e., clearly stated and understood). Teachers could provide students with explicit diagrams or written descriptions of the correct tasks.
- Students will need practice in observing. Being able to focus on a component rather than watching the total action is a learned skill. Students should not be expected to observe more than one criteria at a time.
- The feedback system should be simple for the observer (e.g., plus or minus, thumbs up or thumbs down).
- Peer observation is a valuable tool if criteria for assessment are understood by both the observer and the performer.
- Reminder: The purpose of peer observation is to assist with student learning, not to degrade students or their performance.

SELF-ASSESSMENT

Definition/Description:

The student assessing personal progress as opposed to being assessed by the teacher or by other students. Self-assessments include rating scales for levels of performance, participation, recording performance scores (e.g., distance, accuracy), summary reports after a series of assessment tasks (e.g., dribbling, throwing for accuracy and distance, jump shooting; physical fitness profiles), and questionnaires of likes and dislikes in activities. Self-assessment is a part of logs, journals, and portfolios as students evaluate personal performance or progress toward goals.

Example:

Students are involved in a ropes course activity unit in which they are asked to work together to accomplish group goals. At the completion of the day's activity, each student rates personal progress toward the following: assuming a leadership role, assuming a follower role, assisting someone in the group, working cooperatively with the total group.

Hints for Development and Use:

- Trust your students; they will be very honest in their assessments of themselves.
- Self-assessments provide teachers with insight into students' perceptions and self-concepts as they write summary statements and comments regarding personal performance.
- Students may need guidance in assessing themselves based on past performance and personal goals as opposed to comparisons with standards or others
- Self-assessment can be a valuable tool in helping students accept responsibility for personal

activity and fitness, as well as in setting goals for the development of healthy lifestyle patterns.

WRITTEN TEST

Definition/Description:

Written tests encompass multiple choice, true/false, matching, essay, short answer, and fill-in-the-blank test formats traditionally used to examine knowledge, comprehension, application, analysis, synthesis, and evaluation of the knowledge base in physical education. Broadly speaking, such tests could include other test formats such as oral examinations and examinations that use drawings or pictures to elicit student responses. Written tests are commonly used for short quizzes or for longer formal examinations.

Example:

Physical fitness is a recurring theme throughout public school physical education. The following questions are provided as examples of the various types of questions that might be included on written tests at various grade levels:

K - Primary Grades: Teacher develops a pictorial display of people engaged in various activities ranging from jogging to watching television. Student are examined orally by asking such questions as:

- Teacher points to two pictures, one with a physically active person (jogger) and one with an inactive person (someone reading) and asks the student to choose the picture that shows the person with the fastest beating heart.
- Teacher points to a weight lifter and an jogger and asks which activity is best for building strong muscles.

Middle School to High School: Multiple choice, true/false, matching, and essay questions can be employed when students are able to read at an appropriate level.

- Sue decided to develop her own personal exercise program. Knowing that you were enrolled in PE 101 Physical Fitness Training she asked your advice in developing her program. Referring to the five steps that should be considered in developing personal exercise programs that we discussed in class, what advice would you give to Sue?
- Distinguish between health-related and athletic-related physical fitness. In addition, provide examples of the types of fitness tests used to measure each.
- Which of the equations listed below is commonly used to estimate maximum heart rate?
  a. 220 - weight
  b. 220 - age
  c. 220 - resting heart rate
  d. 220 + resting heart rate
- T/F The optimal training program for developing muscular strength is to lift light weights over many repetitions.
- To improve the physical fitness component known as _____ you should practice stretching exercises.

Hints for Development and Use:

- Written tests should represent a comprehensive sample of the content and behaviors outlined in the instructional objectives. Before writing test questions, a table of specifications or test blueprint outlining the content and behaviors to be elicited by the test can be developed to ensure

that the test represents appropriate content and behaviors.

- Construction of meaningful test questions that reflect appropriate content and elicit appropriate levels of cognition requires practice. Rules for developing test questions can be found in measurement texts such as Safrit and Wood (1995) and Baumgartner and Jackson (1995).
- Students should be made aware of the general content areas covered by a test and the types of questions (e.g., multiple choice or essay) that will be presented.
- Written tests should be developed for the reading and comprehension level of students. Oral presentation of test questions for students in the lower grades or for students with reading difficulties can facilitate the test-taking process.
- Detailed scoring keys are required for essay and short answer tests to increase fairness and objectivity in scoring.

GROUP PROJECT

Definition/Description:

An assessment project completed by several students working cooperatively. As opposed to an event task that can be completed in a single class period, the group project usually takes more than one class period to complete and may include time spent outside of class. Group projects may be performance-based (e.g., presentation of dance, creation of a new game) or involve class presentation of results, displays, wall charts.

Example:

Students are placed in groups of five to six members and are asked to role-play the following scenario: The City Little League coach has asked your group to serve as assistant coaches this season. Specifically, the coach asks you to do a presentation of throwing for varying distances. Each group is instructed to prepare a presentation to include: oral presentation of skills, demonstration of skills, and audiovisuals. Each group member must be part of the presentation. Presentations will be made to the class.

Hints for Development and Use:

- Keep the groups small (four may be the maximum number for some classes).
- Provide guidelines for items that must be included in the project, especially performance skills.
- Within a class, some groups will require assistance to move beyond discussion of detail; others will require assistance to attend to detail.
- The project or game must be complete in itself (i.e., in **final** form).
- The scoring rubric should be shared with students in advance so they are aware of the assessment criteria.
- Keep the project as simple as possible.

PORTFOLIO

Definition/Description:

Portfolios are collections of a student's work assembled over time (Feuer and Fulton, 1993). They include various pieces of evidence documenting student achievement of a goal. Portfolios have been used by artists and models for many years to demonstrate their best work. The focus in student portfolios is on:

- Student thinking

- Growth over time
- Views of oneself as a learner
- Problem-solving

Portfolios should be rated according to their ability to convey to the teacher that the student has met the goals for the class. This should be done concisely. The cover letter that accompanies the portfolio clearly explains why these particular pieces were included (instead of other types of documentation) and how the teacher's goals were met by the student. Criteria should take into consideration the age of the student, the time given for portfolio development, and whether or not the portfolio is being used to fulfill requirements for other teachers and classes.

Examples of portfolio components: *(Note: Not all of these would be included in one portfolio)*

Goal: To learn to play soccer:

- Evidence of playing on a recreational team (e.g., certificate)
- Journal of student successes as skill improved
- Videotape of game play
- A list of the drills practiced three times a week
- A letter from a soccer coach
- A brief review of key rules
- A critique of a soccer game watched discussing various offensive and defensive strategies observed.
- A practice log (e.g., footwork skills) to show improvement in the number that can be done in 30 second time frames
- Chart on skills

Goal: Fitness Development:

- Research paper on training components
- Training log to document distances
- Student diary that describes how he or she felt after each training episode
- A chart that records resting heart rate over time
- Summary paper of the experience
- Log of strength and flexibility activities
  "Before and after" body fat assessments
- An outline of a training program created before the fitness unit began
- A participant's number from a local road race competition
- Pictures
- Journal excerpts
- Graphs of improvement
- The original fitness plan and a corrected plan allowing adjustments for improvement

Examples of portfolio content in sport skill classes:

- Student written self-evaluation of current skill level and individual goals
- Daily log of class activities and individual performance, suggestions for future work
- On-going self, and peer analysis of skill performance and playing performance (checklist, rating scale, criteria-referenced tasks, videotape)
- Based on self-analysis, students select or design appropriate practice program and complete schedule
- Graphs that chart daily practice/play performance on major skills
- Documentation of practice, informal game play and/or organized competition outside of class time
- Set up, conduct, and participate in a tournament or meet, keep group and personal sta-

tistics
- Write a newspaper article reporting on the class tournament as if you were a sports reporter
- Complete and record a play-by-play commentary as if you were a radio or television sports announcer
- Design optional routines according to class rules and practice for competition
- Interview a successful competitor or coach about his or her development and write an article
- Read an autobiography about a successful competitor and write a review
- Write a final analysis of your skill and playing or performing ability, assign your own grade and give rationale
- Write an essay entitled "What I learned and accomplished in _____ . . . and what I learned about myself in the process"
- Generate a reference list of instructional materials
- Attend a clinic, workshop or presentation and write a review

Hints for Development and Use:

- The first step in creating a portfolio involves a teacher decision — determining the desired student outcome or goal. Once this is established and clearly stated, the student can begin gathering evidence that will demonstrate that the goal has been met.
- Portfolios are gathered over time. They may cover 6 to 8 weeks of instruction. Therefore, students need to have adequate time to assemble their information as well as adequate resources. The portfolio is often considered to be assessment in progress. The student has the option of working on components, changing them in ways that students feel make the evidence stronger so that they have achieved the desired goal.
- If a student included every bit of evidence, the portfolio could become massive. Grading these unlimited portfolios would be a monumental if not impossible task. Unlimited portfolios are referred to as working portfolios. For the assessment portfolio, a teacher may limit the portfolio to a certain number of pieces (e.g., seven) and then have the student write a cover letter explaining why the various items were included. Although a teacher may suggest portfolio components or areas to be addressed, the ultimate decision of what is to be included should be left to the student.
- One of the key components of alternative assessment is that the student has ownership and full choice about what is to be included. For instance, let's say a student was learning a psychomotor skill or sport. The teacher thought that a practice log, listing time spent working on the skill was necessary to demonstrate the practice and learning. Instead the student turns in a video showing early game play and game play following practice. The latter piece would also demonstrate skill practice, even though a log of practice time had not been kept. Another example might be if a swimmer included a certificate from the Red Cross documenting completion of a life saving class.
- The teacher must be prepared to accept some unusual forms of documentation in the portfolio. This is not to say that the student always makes the best choice of selection of what to include. A good rubric should explain clearly the intent of the teacher goal, without limiting student creativity to meet the criteria.
- Portfolios are best used when learning involves a complex idea or skill. When many facets and components of learning are involved, it is easier for students to create a portfolio.
- Contents of a portfolio could include the following:
    Report of a group project
    Excerpts from a student's daily journal
    Photo, model, or sketch made by the student
    Notes from an interview or conference
    Teacher-completed checklists
    Copies of awards or prizes
    Video, audio, and computer-generated examples of student work

ROLE PLAYING

Definition/Description:

Students are given a scenario and then asked to simulate the characters they portray or act out the situation that has been set for them. These dialogues can be written or verbalized. Students have the opportunity to portray real world situations. Students are required to use reasoning and problem solving to deal with the reality of the experience as it unfolds.

Examples:

1. Following a wall climbing class, let a student assume the role of Sir Edmond Hillary and discuss how he(she) felt as the summit of Mt. Everest grew closer. Have a student "reporter" interview Sir Edmond.

Note: Rubrics have not been written for these role play examples (see Appendix A, Section 3 for a description of a scoring rubric). The rubric would address the points the teacher felt were important and tried to address with students. The question could have been written differently, and the teacher could have looked at what a student had learned about wall climbing techniques. Another version of the same scenario could have Sir Edmond discussing his training program and conditioning before beginning the trip. Still another could have looked at safety issues. A teacher could have combined two or more of these scenarios into a much broader look at learning.

2. You are at a meeting of the Major League Baseball owners. The topic on the table is league mascots. Some owners want the Indians and Braves to change their symbols. Create the dialogue for the meeting.

3. You are at a local basketball game. Your best friend's sister is on the opposing team. Whenever the team shoots free throws, another friend whistles and makes disruptive noises. Your friend also has been booing officials and is making derogatory remarks to the other team. What would you say to this friend? Create a dialogue for the conversation.

4. You are at a baseball game (Note: you could substitute tennis or racquetball) with a friend from France. This person knows a lot about soccer and basketball, but not much about baseball. How would you explain the rules so that your friend could enjoy the game?

Hints for Development and Use:

- Role playing lends itself easily to cognitive or affective domain assessment. The teacher must be careful to set the stage so that students know what is expected.
- Performing role plays in front of peers may be embarrassing or very difficult for some students. Introduce this activity to students gradually, beginning in small groups without an audience and progressing *gradually* to "performances" for the class. Begin with issues that are familiar to or popular with students before progressing to more personal scenarios.
- The teacher should accept the responses of students in a nonjudgmental way. Students should reflect, paraphrase, and summarize responses that have been given verbally.

EVENT TASK

Definition/Description:

An event task is a performance task that can be completed within 50 minutes. The task is written broadly enough (it is loosely structured) so that there are multiple solutions or many possible correct answers. It should be engaging (capture the interest of the students) and replicate or simulate a real world experience.

Example:

Your group has been asked to organize a half-time show for the local basketball team using the various skills you have developed this year in physical education. Identify the skills you are going to present and create a routine to be performed. Make a list of equipment that you will need, if any. Choose your skills wisely so that everyone in the group is able to perform his or her part of the routine. You may include both individual and group stunts and skills. The performance will last 5 to 6 minutes.

Scoring Criteria:

Score the task a 4 if the students:
- Show variety in their choice of skills
- Choose skills of an appropriate level of difficulty for each member of the group
- Have sufficient skills to last the required time
- Demonstrate an understanding of equipment needs (e.g., tumbling mats, items to juggle, dance music)
- All members of the group are active throughout the routine

Score the task a 3 if the students:
- Show variety in their choice of skills
- Most of the skills are of an appropriate level of difficulty for each member, however, some members are not proficient in everything
- There are enough skills to last the required time
- Equipment needs for the routine are complete and appropriate
- Most members of the group are active throughout the routine, however one or two stand without activity for brief periods

Score the task a 2 if the students:
- Show variety in their choice of skills
- Most of the skills are of an appropriate level of difficulty for each member, however, there are several errors caused by students trying to do things that are too difficult
- The routine lasts about 4 1/2 minutes
- Equipment needs for the routine are complete and appropriate
- Most of the time everyone is active, however, there are places in the routine that are dominated by the most skilled performers

Score the task a 1 if the students:
- Use the same skills repetitively
- Have frequent errors caused by doing things that are too difficult
- The routine is very short
- Some of the necessary equipment has been omitted from the list
- Are active much of the time but the whole group does little together
- Do not have a good flow to the routine

Score the task a 0 if the students:
- Do things individually instead of having designed a routine

Score the task blank if the students:
- Do not do a routine

Hints for Development and Use:

A performance event should:
- Solicit responses representing all proficiency levels if possible
- Require minimal to no interaction with the person administering the test
- Result in individual responses that can be scored
- Allow variable student grouping (two to four students)
- Be completed within 50 minutes
- Have all materials necessary for successful completion readily available to students

OBSERVATION - TEACHER/STUDENT

Definition/Description:

Teacher observation is the most utilized form of assessment in physical education. Teachers observe students on a regular basis as part of the instructional process. Teacher observation can also be used more systematically to provide objective data on student performance to collect information on the instructional process or to evaluate students. All students or a sample of students representing different skill levels can be assessed. There are many tools that teachers can use to record observational data including anecdotal records, checklists, rating scales, or scoring rubrics. All of these tools can be used whether in live observation or with video analysis. They can be used by the teacher or by the student in peer assessment or self-assessment. The value of the information recorded in each of these cases is enhanced if teachers have a clear idea of what they are looking for in their observations and attend to issues related to the reliability and validity of the data they collect.

Anecdotal Record: The teacher establishes broad categories of concern and then takes notes on everything that is observed in relation to those categories. Notes are usually kept in the form of a log or running description and are usually nonevaluative.

Example: The teacher is interested in observing how students integrate mainstreamed students into their group work. During a group assignment the teacher records the interaction of mainstreamed students in various groups.

Observational record: Xavia did not go to the area of the gym with the rest of her group. One student from the group noticed that she was not part of the group and went over to get her. Thomas was included immediately in the group and given the assignment by the group to work with one of the more highly skilled students. Jose just wandered the gym until the teacher brought him to his assigned group.

Checklist: Checklists are usually used to determine whether a student meets or does not meet a particular criteria. The teacher checks off when a student meets the criteria.

Example: The teacher checks off when a student meets each of the criteria for an overhand throw.

Observational record:
- Steps with the opposite foot
- Sequential rotation
- Elbow out and back
- Forearm lag

Rating Scale: Rating scales are used to determine the degree to which identified criteria have been met in an observation. The teacher designates a) the important components of behavior to

be assessed and b) the levels of performance desired to be discriminated.

Example: The teacher has decided to systematically observe the degree to which students comply with class rules. Several students each class period are targeted for observation.

Observational record: For each class rule the teacher records one of the following levels of performance:

   1= No incidence of noncompliance are observed
   2= One incidence of noncompliance is observed
   3= More than one incidence of noncompliance are observed but student is primarily compliant
   4= Student is more often noncompliant than compliant

Scoring Rubric: Scoring rubrics are in one sense rating scales that use multiple criteria simultaneously. The teacher establishes desired levels of performance and then defines the criteria that are essential for each of those levels of performance. See Appendix A, Section 3 for additional information regarding scoring rubrics.

Example: The teacher wants to evaluate offensive game play in a three vs. three soccer game using a goalie.

Observational record:

Level 1:
   • Passes ahead of receiver
   • Moves into a logical empty space when receiving
   • Maintains possession until defended

Level 2:
   • Usually passes ahead of the receiver
   • Moves into empty space to receive but not always logically in relation to the defense
   • Does not always wait for defense before getting rid of the ball

Level 3:
   • Passes are more often not ahead of the receiver
   • Does not move into an empty space to receive the ball
   • The decision to pass is not made in relation to the defender

Video analysis: All of the techniques for observation included above can be used either live or with the help of video analysis. Teachers and students can use video in time outside of class or during class. Video analysis has the advantage of slow motion capability that is useful for many skills that are too fast to be accurately analyzed via live observation. Video analysis also has the advantage of being replayed to increase the reliability of the observation. Teachers who do not have the luxury of evaluating each student during class time can use video analysis to get very complete and accurate information of the performance of individuals. Video analysis is also extremely useful to assess the degree to which program objectives and goals have been accomplished. Often teachers who see their classes on videotape are able to see a lot more when the responsibility for instruction is removed.

Example 1: The teacher videotapes all of the final games of a sport unit and establishes a scoring rubric based on the degree to which students use the individual skills of the game, know and use the rules, and use the game strategies that have been taught.

Example 2: The teacher sets up a corner of the gym for videotaping of a skill that has been taught. Each student takes a turn videotaping his or her performance in this skill. The teacher goes through the tape to indicate the counter number associated with the location on the tape of each student's performance. The teacher puts the tape in the school media center and requires each student to use a rating scale to assess his or her own performance and to determine what aspects of performance need improvement.

Hints for Development and Use:

- Establish specific criteria for observation ahead of time so that you know what you are looking for and how you are going to observe.
- Choose a method of recording and plan an observation record that is easy to use.
- Do not try to look at too many criteria at one time.
- A lot of useful information can be obtained by sampling students rather than trying to observe every student every period. If all students need to be observed, choose several a day as your focus. If you are using observation for instructional feedback or program assessment, choose students who are likely to be at different levels of performance as what you are observing.
- When you need a high degree of reliability and validity for your assessment, practice using your criteria until you can use them consistently in a variety of contexts.

Appendix B: Resources

Baker EL: Making performance assessment work: the road ahead. *Educational Leadership*, 51(6): 58-62, 1994.

Bartz D, Anderson-Robinson S, and Hillman L: Performance assessment: make them show what they know. *Principal*, 73(3): 11-14, 1994.

Baumgartner TA and Jackson AS: *Measurement for evaluation in physical education and exercise science* , 5 ed, Dubuque, IA, 1995, Wm. C. Brown.

Brickell B et al: *Designing assessments: applications for physical education.* Willow Street, PA, PSAHPERD, 1994, P.E. - L.I.F.E. Project.

Collins DR and Hodges PB: *A comprehensive guide to sports skills tests and measurement.* Springfield, IL, 1978, C. Thomas.

Cunningham G: *Assessment in the classroom: constructing and interpreting tests.* New York, Macmillan (in press).

Feuer M and Fulton K: The many faces of performance assessment. *Phi Delta Kappan*, 74(6): 478, 1993.

Hensley LD, Morrow JR, and East WB: Practical measurement to solve practical problems. *Journal of Physical Education, Recreation and Dance*, 61(3): 42-44, 1990.

Herman J, Aschbacker P, and Winters L: *A practical guide to alternative Aassessment.* Alexandria, VA, 1992, Association for Supervision and Curriculum Development.

Kneer ME (ed) et al: *"Basic stuff" series.* Reston, VA 1981, AAHPERD.

Marzano R, Pickering, D, and McTighe J: *Assessing student outcomes.* Alexandria, VA, 1993, Association for Supervision and Curriculum Development.

McGee R and Farrow A: *Test questions for physical education activities.* Champaign, IL, 1987, Human Kinetics.

Meyer CA: What's the difference between authentic and performance assessment? *Educational Leadership*, 49(8): 39, 1992.

Perrone V: *Expanding student assessment.* Alexandria, VA, 1991, Association for Supervision and Curriculum Development.

Pierson CA and Beck SS: Performance assessment: the realities that will reflect the rewards. *Childhood Education,* 70(1): 29-32, 1993.

Safrit MJ:*Complete guide to youth fitness testing.* Champaign, IL, 1995, Human Kinetics.

Safrit MJ and Wood TM: *Introduction to measurement in physical education and exercise science* (3 ed). St Louis, 1995, Mosby.

Schick J: Written tests in activity classes. *Journal of Physical Education Recreation and Dance,* 52(4): 21-22, 83, 1981.

Stiehl J: Becoming responsible—Theoretical and practical considerations.*Journal of Physical Education, Recreation and Dance,* May-June, 38-40 +,1993.

Stiggins R, Conklin N, and Bridgeford M: Classroom assessment: a key to effective education. *Educational Measurement: Issues and Practice,* 5(2): 5-17, 1986.

Strand BN and Wilson R: *Assessing sport skills.* Champaign, IL, 1993, Human Kinetics.

Thomson JR: Multicultural education: Culturally responsive teaching, introduction. *Journal of Physical Education, Recreation and Dance,* November-December, 31-32, 1994.

Wiggins G: A true test: toward more authentic and equitable assessment. *Phi Delta Kappan,* 69(9): 703-713, 1989.

Wiggins G: Assessment: authenticity, context, and validity. *Phi Delta Kappan,* 75(3): 200-214, 1993.

Wood TM: *Evaluation and testing: the road less traveled.* In Silverman S and Ennis C(eds): *Enhancing learning in physical education: a research approach to effective teaching.* Champaign, IL, Human Kinetics (in press).

Worthen BR: Is your school ready for alternative assessment? *Phi Delta Kappan,* 74(6): 455-456, 1993.